Lucas Malet

Colonel Enderby's wife

Vol. II

Lucas Malet

Colonel Enderby's wife
Vol. II

ISBN/EAN: 9783337043797

Printed in Europe, USA, Canada, Australia, Japan

Cover: Foto ©ninafisch / pixelio.de

More available books at **www.hansebooks.com**

COLONEL ENDERBY'S WIFE

A NOVEL

BY

LUCAS MALET

AUTHOR OF
"MRS. LORIMER, A SKETCH IN BLACK AND WHITE"

"Lequel de nous n'a sa terre promise, son jour d'extase, et sa fin dans l'exil?"—AMIEL

IN THREE VOLUMES
VOL. II.

LONDON
KEGAN PAUL, TRENCH & CO., 1, PATERNOSTER SQUARE
1885

CONTENTS OF VOL. II.

BOOK THIRD.
LOVER AND MISTRESS.
(*Continued.*)

CHAPTER		PAGE
V.	Episodes in the Life of a Negative Saint	3
VI.	Two Ways of True Love	29
VII.	The Colonel clasps Hands with his Fate	50
VIII.	Eleanor tries to break her Chain ...	57
IX.	"Peu de gens savent être vieux"	69
X.	Mrs. Murray decides to put down her Foot	89

BOOK FOURTH.
THE PROMISED LAND.

I.	Question and Answer	119
II.	Mrs. Pierce-Dawnay grows Suspicious of her Handiwork	135

CHAPTER		PAGE
III.	In which Malvolio does the Honours of the Villa Mortelli	150
IV.	Telling of Leisure, of Love, and of a Sunday Evening	168

BOOK FIFTH.
IN SUSPENSE.

I.	Jessie answers a Question	197
II.	The Shadow of a Great Fear	216
III.	Colonel Enderby makes his Choice	227
IV.	Dr. Symes finds a Clue	250
V.	Romance at a Disadvantage	268
VI.	"For Auld Lang Syne"	288

BOOK THIRD.
LOVER AND MISTRESS.
(Continued.)

COLONEL ENDERBY'S WIFE.

CHAPTER V.

EPISODES IN THE LIFE OF A NEGATIVE SAINT.

As Mr. Ames had said of her, Cecilia Farrell, *née* Murray, had a positive genius for doing her duty. From this statement it may be gathered that her temperament was neither a conspicuously artistic nor a conspicuously original one. I make the above comment not without a movement of hesitancy and a trembling of the inner man. For the word Duty has come to be the shibboleth of the virtuous English in so eminent a degree, that any person using it lightly, and with an implication of possible limits to its supreme worth and value, runs the risk of finding himself written down as a somewhat dangerous and disreputable character.

But indeed, the saving grace of Duty has been so belauded, so praised, and insisted upon, that by now it surely must be uplifted above all fear of detraction. It is the pole-star of the Anglo-Saxon night. We all steer by it—or by what we reckon to be it—and demand that others shall steer by it too. It appears to be set far above in the heavens, immovable, everlasting. It is a name to conjure with; a fetish to appease; a city of refuge when argument threatens to fail. And perhaps the most engaging quality about this same idea of duty is, that everybody can look at it from their own point of view, use its power in support of their own cause, invoke the mystic benefit of its name in the most opposite cases. One may even go one step further, and admit frankly that the great practical use of such a recognized watchword as Duty is that the using of it alone is sufficient, and that, having used it, you are then agreeably free to do what you please. Cerberus has got his sop. Go on your way rejoicing. By the majority, nothing further will be required of you.

Only here and there will you come across some sincere and simple soul, who having been indoctrinated with the conception of Duty, takes it home to his or her heart, and tries faithfully to work it out in daily life—a somewhat silly and innocent proceeding no doubt, grounded on an absence of the powers of observation and generalization. This simplicity of mind, however, is becoming more and more infrequent. It takes its rise in an abnormal development of the conscience; and may be described as a sense of universal obligation towards the disagreeable. It is the occasion of much tyranny in unscrupulous persons, and affords but a limited source of joy to the possessor of it, since he is almost always struggling to conform to a shifting ideal of conduct prescribed by others. It induces a spirit as far away from the strong inward compelling of the artist, or the luminous calm of the philosopher, as anything very well can. It distorts and confuses the reason, and rubs down all the sharp edges of the individuality. It takes away all inspiring sense of freedom, and leaves the poor soul wandering through a dim world, the sport of circumstance, and of many, but most untrustworthy guides.

It may be asserted of Cecilia Farrell, I think, that she belonged to this rare, admirable, and somewhat depressing type of humanity. Her over-mastering sense of duty had caused her to be the prey first of one person, and then of another. It had prevented her abandoning herself freely to any one emotion, it had kept her in a constant attitude of self-restraint and self-repression. Life had been but an attenuated and dust-coloured affair to her. She had habitually come in only for the second best, for meagre satisfactions, and sorrows that were far from being as robust and full-bodied as sorrows should be. Both her pains and pleasures had been set in a low key. Some women would have found a very sufficient opportunity for rich drama in passages of Cecilia's career. But in her case conscience was supreme, and its action was paralyzing. The question of what she ought to feel usurped the position of what she actually did feel, and cast a dreary blight over all her emotions.

And then, the worst of it is, such a woman gets so little sympathy. A half-starved, quiet, inglorious existence, such as Mrs. Farrell's, is simply uninteresting to society at large. People generally referred to her with regretful, almost condemnatory inflection, as "poor Cecilia." Mrs. Farrell knew this; she hardly resented it. As time went on she grew to accept the definition unreservedly. She became "poor Cecilia" to herself; and this not with any lingering of sentimental self-pity. The adjective had still a touch of reprobation in it. She felt that she was very far from being a success; that she was a slightly inconvenient adjunct both to her own and to her husband's families—a person who never had given, or was likely to give, cause for exuberant congratulations.

Duty had dried her girlish tears for young Philip Enderby. It had compelled her, at her mother's desire, to accept Eugene

Farrell. To accept not only the honourable prefix to his name, which filled Mrs. Murray with such lively self-glorification, but to accept also his many debts, his uncertain humours, his ceaseless wanderings from one foreign watering-place to another, ostensibly in search of health, actually in search of "play." Duty had made her ignore a very undeniable amount of indifference, neglect, exactingness, if nothing worse, on his part; for Eugene was not a wholly pleasant person to live with. It made her get over the tender sorrow caused by the deaths of two little babies, who, after the briefest experience of the doubtfully joyful life of this planet, decided to leave it for a more peaceful and congenial atmosphere. It made her shed tears for her husband on much the same principle as that which had dried them for her lover long ago. Finally, it made her bow her patient neck under Mrs. Murray's not easy yoke, and obey spiritually, while she supported materially, that well-preserved and still vigorous old woman. As Mrs. Pierce-Dawnay had said, Cecilia always was more or less of a fool; and as Mr.

Ames had replied, she was undoubtedly a good one.

Mrs. Farrell's income had never been large, and her husband's comforts and amusements naturally stood first in the list of necessary expenses. There is something lowering to a woman of gentle birth and refined feeling in struggling with grasping hotel-keepers and foreign servants—whose respect is carefully regulated by the size of your rooms, and the floor on which they are situated. At the time when Cecilia Farrell met Colonel Enderby at the little red villa, her eyes had grown anxious under the many difficulties and provocations of her lot. Her complexion was by no means good; her hair had lost all trace of youthful brightness, and was freely streaked with grey. Her features, always large, had lost the softness of youth, and had become too distinctly emphasized. Her whole face had crystallized into an habitual expression of resigned discomfort—untouched, however, with fretfulness. Many well-bred Englishwomen—and Cecilia could lay claim to very good breeding on her father's side, at all events—present a singular resemblance to young turkey pullets. Mrs. Farrell, with her small head, prominent nose, sloping shoulders, tall flat figure, and general want of generous development, reminded one forcibly of one of those ladylike, but somewhat distressed-looking birds. You recognized the fact that she was a good woman, and what is technically described as a lady; but you had a hankering after the cheerful insolent self-confidence, and finely rounded contours of women, either a little above or a little below her in the social scale.

It has been hinted that Cecilia Farrell's married life was not a conspicuously happy one, and that her husband's conduct towards her left something to be desired; still it is only fair to add that, possibly, the fault was not exclusively on Eugene's side. Cecilia's virtues were not of the order calculated to make her a lively and sparkling companion, and Mr. Farrell was a gentleman of many moods, some of them almost regrettably lively. It is a melancholy admission, yet a less excellent woman would probably have had more power for good over Eugene Farrell. Like so many excellent women, Cecilia's sense of humour was radically defective; she took life hard and anxiously —was almost equally alarmed by her husband's fits of depression and by his fits of gaiety. She soon grew to be an irritation, a weariness, to her light-hearted, mercurial lord and master. She represented all the virtuous, tedious side of life to him. In short, he was horribly bored with her.

One day, sitting in the garden of the *Palais Royal*, some eighteen months after his marriage, a bright idea came to Eugene Farrell. He had gone through a painful scene with his wife the night before, after making some certainly not very creditable disclosures to her on the subject of recent losses at *rouge et noir*. The summer breeze rustled the leaves of the little plane trees, and made merry with the long ribbon streamers of the *bonnes'* white caps. Dust and miscellaneous shreds of paper whirled up in a purposeless dance off the brown gravel, and then sank to rest again. Eugene Farrell curled up the ends of his fair moustache; watched a nurse struggling with a couple of refractory children; treated a smart young person, with remarkably high-heeled boots, to a somewhat comprehensive stare as she passed in front of him; then smiled and slapped his thigh gently, as though he had arrived at the solution of a difficult problem.

"Cecilia grows inconvenient," he said to himself,—quite good-humouredly. "She shall return to the condition of primitive woman. She has all the makings of a capital beast of burden in her. She shall walk behind, and carry the cooking-pot and the tent-poles."

He went back to his hotel, and began forthwith to put his bright idea into execution. It saved him a world of trouble, it is true; yet it may be questioned whether it made Cecilia a much happier woman, or Eugene a much better man.

It is unnecessary to follow the course of poor Mrs. Farrell's matrimonial infelicities further. Suffice it to say that, inspired by the paramount obligation of duty, she obeyed her husband irreproachably; bewailed him when he departed this life,—clad in the requisite quantity of crape;—and, since the attitude of primitive woman had through habit become so very natural to her, willingly offered herself as beast of burden to her mother and her son.

On the morning following his entertainment by Jessie Pierce-Dawnay, Master Johnnie Farrell demanded that his mother should take him out-of-doors at a comparatively early hour. The nurse, who should have been his companion, was assisting in the mysteries and intricacies of Mrs. Murray's toilette. The boy wanted, he said, to go down to the beach; so Cecilia, of course, prepared herself to comply with his desires.

He was a pretty child, with a round head, bright brown hair, and rather broad features; quick, eager, light-hearted, moody—like his father. His disposition was good, as his doting yet anxious mother told herself twenty times a day. Whether it was likely to be improved by jealous worship and absence of discipline, was a question she did not ask. Probably, at six years old,

Eugene Farrell's disposition had been good too.

Johnnie teased to be taken down on to the beach till he got into the hotel garden; and then he suddenly changed his mind. The Grand Hotel at Terzia was new in those days, and its garden was of very simple construction. A square plot of ground, with the hotel buildings round three sides of it, fronting on the street, from which it was divided by high and ornate iron railings. Four large raised beds, planted with palms, and bordered with flowers; a couple of stone fountains on opposite sides, each with two broad basins, the upper one supported by three voracious-looking, open-mouthed dolphins; and for the rest, gravel paths, gas-lamps, and an innumerable company of yellow iron chairs set in long lines, bordering the pathways, and waiting—usually vainly—for occupants. Behind the flat-roofed painted hotel, with its wide balcony, rows of yellow shutters and red and grey awnings, the hills tower up in a quaint conical outline against the deep blue of the sky.

When Mrs. Farrell and her boy came into the garden, it was glary with sunshine, save where the left wing of the buildings cast a sharp-edged blue shadow to the ground. The long leaves of the palms rattled in the wind, alive with the breath of the mountains and the sea. The windows of the restaurant on the ground floor stood wide open. There was an invigorating crispness, sparkle, and freshness in the morning.

Johnnie Farrell, espying the stone basins of the fountains, quite forgot his longing after the beach.

"I say, mother, we'll stay here," he announced authoritatively. "I'll sail boats. It's better for my boats than the sea. Those plaguey old waves are so big, you know; and then, you're always bothering about my getting wet."

Mrs. Farrell dragged a yellow iron chair out of the rank into the cool shade, and sat down submissively. She had tucked up her petticoats pretty high, with the cleanly if ungraceful instinct of an Englishwoman who is going for a walk. She had also put on stout boots, the upper leathers of which were somewhat crumpled across the toes, and a large turned-down hat, surrounded by a forlorn arrangement in green gauze veils. Her circumstances prescribed a black dress, and her natural modesty an over-jacket—both articles somewhat limp in substance and uncertain in cut. In her hand she held a large white covered umbrella, the outward purity of which had suffered considerably from the action of rain, and from contact with various foreign objects. Undoubtedly, at this moment, Mrs. Farrell in appearance realized very completely the modern idea of the pilgrim and sojourner. She looked pre-eminently not at home.

For the best part of ten minutes Johnnie was completely absorbed in the voyages of his boats across the clear water, under the noses of the vicious-looking dolphins. His mother sat watching him, throwing in a word of warning, now and again, as he leaned dangerously far over the curled lip of the stone basin. Moments such as these were quite the happiest of her life. She had her boy all to herself. She was half ashamed of her own delight in watching his neat little figure and active movements. On this particular morning he looked specially engaging in a clean blue-and-white linen suit, and broad-brimmed hat. Cecilia leaned back in her yellow iron chair. Life for the moment was sweet; it was uncomplicated.

But Master Johnnie speedily tired of his boats, and began to search further a-field for entertainment.

"I say, mother," he cried out suddenly, "there's the man who was up at Jessie's last night. He's going to have his breakfast in the window just behind you. I shall go and have a talk with him."

Mrs. Farrell's gracious sense of the sweetness of life passed away with a flash.

"No, Johnnie; don't," she answered quite sharply. "I don't wish you to."

The boy stared for a moment at his mother. He was unaccustomed to such peremptory prohibitions.

"Grandmamma says I'm not to talk to waiters, because they are not gentlemen.

Isn't he a gentleman?" he inquired, after a moment's reflection.

The high treble notes of the child's voice were very audible, and the open window of the restaurant was directly behind her. Poor Cecilia moved nervously on her chair, and her thin face went crimson.

"Hush, hush!" she answered. "We'll go away now. We'll go down to the beach. You'd like to go down to the beach now, wouldn't you, darling?"

But the darling, unfortunately, was possessed of an inquiring mind.

"I want to know why I mayn't go and talk to that man," he repeated.

He stood in front of Cecilia, with his feet planted well apart, his hat well on the back of his head, and an alarming expression of alertness in his small countenance.

"He seemed to me a very civil sort of fellow," he added, with a little critical air, which would have tickled anybody but his poor mother.

"Be quiet, Johnnie," she said, getting up in a condition of the liveliest embarrassment. "You're very tiresome and naughty."

"No, I'm not," he responded promptly. "It's naughty to wet my feet, and it's naughty to take off my hat in the sun. I haven't done either."

After which concise statement of the moral code, the boy took a few steps to the right, from whence he could command a full view of the window, and the table on which Galli was silently setting out Colonel Enderby's breakfast.

"Hullo, I say; good morning!" he called out to the Colonel, who stood with his back to the window, trying—rather vainly—to interest himself in his letters. "Mother won't tell me why, but she says I oughtn't to speak to you."

"Johnnie, Johnnie, why are you so naughty? Pray, pray don't!" exclaimed Mrs. Farrell, red, piteous, and distracted.

Philip Enderby had come down to breakfast feeling very far from cheerful. He had, at considerable cost, done what he believed to be right; and yet his mental attitude was by no means self-congratulatory. He was suffering from the moral collapse which almost invariably follows on strong moral effort. He was not so much tempted to regret his past action, to go back on what he had done, as to sink into a state of apathy and indifference. The colour had gone out of life; it had turned dull and leaden, heavy, uninspiring. Yesterday the world had been touched with poetry. To-day the poetry was gone, and everything had become very commonplace and mechanical. Then, too, the prospect of an interview with Mrs. Murray was far from agreeable to him. Philip had not attempted to analyze the sensations produced in his mind by his meeting with Cecilia, but he knew very well that the whole affair was extremely awkward and uncomfortable.

Among his letters was a good-natured gossipy epistle from his sister-in-law, Mrs. Jack Enderby. As he read it, Philip's heart warmed towards his old home and his own country. He believed he was tired of the excitement of the last fortnight; he longed to get back to less intricate and more normal feelings and surroundings. He was in the act of framing an excuse by which, a few days hence, he might dissolve travelling partnership with Mr. Drake—who was awaiting his arrival at Spezia, preparatory to starting for Venice—and journey back to the refreshing monotony of Bassett Darcy, when little Johnnie Farrell's shrill voice caused him to turn suddenly to the window.

"Oh! good morning, young man," he said kindly. He could not help feeling a certain interest in the child. "You are not afraid of me this morning, then?"

"Of course I'm not," answered the boy, with a show of dignity. "I'm not so silly as to be afraid of anything by daylight."

Poor Cecilia, meanwhile, was suffering a small martyrdom. She was embarrassed enough on her own account, added to which she was in a fever of nervousness as to what Master Johnnie might elect to say next. She had moved a little aside, and stood in the full blaze of the pitiless sunshine, helplessly holding her large umbrella, and looking a lamentably distressed and dowdy British female, as

Colonel Enderby stepped out on to the gravel, holding out his hand to the little boy.

"That's capital," he said, smiling, "never to be afraid of anything in the daylight."

With the fatal impulse of a very shy person, Mrs. Farrell thereupon rushed wildly into speech.

"Oh! please don't let Johnnie bother you," she began. "You were just going to breakfast; don't let him keep you. We are going down to the sea. It is such a fine morning, that I brought him out early. It was very kind of you to promise to go and see my mother. She will be so glad to see you. She will be ready any time after half-past eleven—at least, I believe she will be ready by then. I am afraid I may not be in; but the number of our sitting-room is ninety-six, on the right—no, on the left, I mean—of the staircase."

Cecilia Farrell undoubtedly presented a sorry spectacle to her former lover. She had not been a very effective person at any time, and a constant carrying of cooking-pots and tent-poles had by no means increased her power of taking the stage well.

Philip Enderby was chivalrous. It pained him to see any woman, and specially this particular woman, at a disadvantage.

"Oh, thanks; I shall find my way," he answered. Then he added, looking good-naturedly down at the pretty boy, "I am sorry I am leaving here to-day. If I had stayed longer this young gentleman and I might have made better acquaintance. I dare say we should find a lot to say to each other. I'm afraid I presented myself to him in rather a disagreeable light last night."

"He was over-excited last night," began Mrs. Farrell, catching wildly at another subject. "He had been playing all the afternoon in the sun. I like spending Sunday quietly. I don't quite approve of going out on Sunday. We might just as well have stayed in Genoa yesterday, and gone to see the Pierce-Dawnays to-day. But my mother wished to go yesterday, and so, of course, I could not object."

She made this confession with admirable simplicity.

As has already been hinted, Colonel Enderby was a little on edge. He gave way to a movement of irritation.

"You still consult other people's inclinations before your own, Mrs. Farrell," he said.

"I say, there's the tram stopping," interrupted Johnnie; "and there's that maid of Jessie's; do you see, mother? I don't like her. She called me a troublesome spoilt baby yesterday. I'm not spoilt, and I'm not a baby, am I now, mother?"

As the boy spoke, Parker descended from the tramcar. The conductor, too, got down off his little platform at the back, and stood aside, waiting politely, as for the passage of some person of recognized distinction. Then Mrs. Pierce-Dawnay emerged from within the vehicle, gave the smiling conductor a royal sort of bow in passing, gathered her black mantle tight down over her handsome bust and shoulders, swept in at the iron gates and up the broad gravel drive, into the middle of the hotel garden.

"Oh, I say, mother, if that maid of Jessie's is coming here, I shan't stay. I shall go down to the beach right slick off, you know."

Master Johnnie Farrell, in the course of his wanderings about the continent of Europe, had acquired a directness of intention and a power of expression decidedly beyond his years.

Eleanor looked extremely well as she walked up the garden. There was an entire indifference to observation, and a certain concentration of purpose in her appearance which was impressive.

"Come along, mother, let's go down to the beach," said the child, pulling petulantly at his mother's stringy skirts.

Eleanor, who was nearly opposite to the group by the restaurant window, suddenly turned her head.

"Ah! you are there!" she exclaimed quickly, coming towards Colonel Enderby.

Her face was pale, almost sallow; her brown eyes seemed sunk, and there were dark circles round them. She looked worn and aged. Mrs. Farrell, with a woman's quick reading of the outward signs of trouble, said to herself wonderingly,—" Why, she has been crying."

"I want to see you at once, Colonel Enderby. I must talk to you. I have something important to say," Mrs. Pierce-Dawnay went on as she came nearer to him. She hardly noticed Cecilia Farrell.

"I say, though, you know, he hasn't had his breakfast yet," remarked the little boy.

Eleanor shrugged her shoulders slightly.

"Ah! that dear child again."

"I am quite at your service," Philip returned courteously.

The lady, he thought, looked capable of developing dangerous energy if she was kept waiting. He did not care very much about his breakfast just then, neither did he care very much for Mrs. Pierce-Dawnay's visit, for that matter. He had delivered his *ultimatum:* he wanted to get away; he did not in the least wish to re-open the question. And what on earth could she want with him? It was a nuisance her surging down upon him in this violent sort of way. But then, everything was a disgusting nuisance this morning. Standing talking, or rather trying to talk, to Mrs. Farrell in the sunshine without his hat was a nuisance of the first water. You will observe that Colonel Enderby was by no means in an heroic frame of mind.

"We'll go, Johnnie," said Cecilia. She was rather sore at heart.

The Colonel's last speech seemed to imply something of a reproach, and she was particularly susceptible to reproaches. She disliked Mrs. Pierce-Dawnay too—chiefly, I imagine, because she was afraid of her. She would get quit of these people, and be alone with her boy.

Parker meanwhile stood a tall black column, in the centre of the hotel garden.

"I must speak to you alone," said Mrs. Pierce-Dawnay. "Parker, go somewhere and sit down and wait. Pah!" she added irritably, "how abominably stupid everybody is to-day! That *enfant terrible* of Mrs. Farrell's is not coming back, I trust?

We will go inside here, Colonel Enderby. You can have your breakfast, and I will talk to you. It is simply scorching out-of-doors."

CHAPTER VI.

TWO WAYS OF TRUE LOVE.

Mrs. Pierce-Dawnay sat down just opposite to Colonel Enderby at the other side of the table on which his breakfast was laid, in the window of the restaurant. She untied the ribbons of her mantle at the neck, and flung it impatiently off her shoulders. She unbuttoned her long *Suède* gloves, and, drawing them off, threw them down on the table before her. She pushed her chair a little back into the soft shadow of the white curtained casement.

"Begin—eat," she said imperatively, looking across at her companion. "I can talk to you just as well so, and it will look more natural if any one passes."

It is all very well to say "Begin—eat;" but how on earth is a man of ordinary sensibility, still more a man suffering a reaction after considerable mental excitement—how is he calmly to dissect a nicely browned sole, and inquire into the inner mysteries of a hen's egg, when a woman with such an intense and tragic countenance is sitting opposite to and watching him?

"Really," said Colonel Enderby, with a feeling something between amusement and annoyance—" really, I think you would find it more comfortable up in the *salon*. My breakfast can very well wait."

"No," she answered quickly; "I prefer this. Give me a cup of coffee, if you like, to keep up appearances; but go on with your breakfast. I assure you, it will be best."

Philip gave her a cup of coffee, and sat down again. A man with his mouth full of fried fish is at a disadvantage, unquestionably; but then, what could he do?

Mrs. Pierce-Dawnay was conscious of being a little beside herself. She needed all the support she could get from outside things. This public situation, the unromantic associations of knives and forks, hot rolls, little tables, and all the rest of it, would help her to maintain her self-control. She leant forward and stirred her coffee, speaking all the while rapidly, almost as though reciting a lesson learned by heart.

"You told me you were obliged to go away to-day. You refused to tell me what reasons compelled you to go. I think I have arrived at those reasons. They do great honour to your delicacy of feeling, but they are based upon a mistake. I have come here this morning to entreat you, most earnestly, to reconsider your decision."

Eleanor did not raise her head, but she glanced up at him for a moment, from under her dark eyebrows. The oval of her face was very perfect, as she held her head in this position. Her lips were slightly compressed; but that perhaps only increased the beauty of her mouth. She was evidently trying hard to keep herself in hand. A strange expression in her eyes and the restless action of her hands alone betrayed her inward agitation.

"I should not have trusted to my own

opinion in this matter," she continued, without giving Philip time to make any rejoinder; "but another person thinks as I do, and that decided me to come to you. You must remember, I have already warned you that foreign ways are different to English ones—this must be my excuse for speaking to you plainly, and without further circumlocution. We may be in error as to your reasons. In that case, you have only to tell me so. I shall not resent, though I shall certainly regret it."

Eleanor paused. Philip Enderby had laid down his knife and fork; he leant back in his chair. He knew quite well what she was going to say. Again the queer paralyzing conviction that all this had happened to him before—which had haunted him on the day of his first visit to the Villa Mortelli—took possession of him. It was distressing, yet he could not break away from it. His will seemed in a state of suspension. He must let her speak, and what would happen, happen. He was powerless alike to hasten or prevent the course of events.

"If," said Eleanor, keeping her eyes

fixed on the rim of her coffee-cup—" if, Colonel Enderby, you have any peculiar interest in my step-daughter, if you prefer her—— Oh, how shall I put it? If—will you pardon my saying it bluntly?—you are in love with her, don't go away. Stay. You have my leave to do so. There is no man on earth to whom I would more willingly give Jessie than to you."

Philip leant his elbows on the table and covered his face with his hands. All the thwarted yearning, worship, desire, which had left him last night so sad and hungry, rushed into his soul again. He was a strong man; but he shook like a leaf at that moment.

Eleanor sat up. She watched him keenly and anxiously. After a few seconds she spoke again, in the same low voice.

"I have tried, believe me, to do my duty by my husband's child; but a time has come when it would be better, far better, for both of us, that she should pass into stronger and safer keeping than mine. And in whose keeping would she be so safe as in yours—her father's and my best and truest friend? And Jessie, surely, is a very fair trust to offer any man? She is very lovely, and gay, and sweet-tempered. She is very winning; she seems to carry the sunshine itself in her smile. Her charm and brightness are all her own: if she has any faults," Eleanor went on slowly, "they are of my making. I have not always been very wise with her, poor child."

Colonel Enderby looked at his companion as she said these last few words. She sat staring in front of her, and her face was very sad. The growing alienation, all the harshness and bitterness of her feeling towards Jessie, during the past year, rushed into her mind. There had been moments when she had come near absolutely hating the young girl. She was still smarting from her interview of the night before with Bertie Ames. She had come to the Colonel that morning in a storm of jealousy, of revenge, of wounded self-love, and of genuine fear too. She wanted to save Jessie quite as urgently as she wanted to save herself.

Things had reached a pass in which silence and denial were no longer possible to Philip

Enderby. He had to face the situation and admit it.

"Tell me, Mrs. Pierce-Dawnay," he said at last, gravely and quietly, "can you honestly say that I am a fitting husband for a beautiful girl of twenty? I am eight-and-forty; every year will make me sensibly older. I have not a large fortune; I have not a distinguished position, or brilliant future to offer a woman. My fighting days are, in all probability, over; younger men, men of the modern school, are crowding forward in my profession, and we old-fashioned soldiers are pretty well out of it, so I have practically no career before me. Dare I, have I any right to, go to a woman, in the first flush of her youth and beauty—she has so much to give—go to her like this, with my hands empty?"

Eleanor turned to him swiftly. Their eyes met. She looked him full in the face.

"If you love her—yes," she said.

Philip Enderby took a long, deep breath. He pushed away his chair and stood up. A necessity for movement was upon him. Just then the glad sea-wind blew back the half-

closed shutter of the southern window of
the restaurant, and the sunshine streamed
in aslant the large light room, flooding the
spot where he stood. Something more than
sunlight illumined the Colonel's face at the
moment. It was radiant with the flame of
a great and beautiful passion. His eyes
were misty with tears.

"Love her?" he cried, with a strange,
short laugh—"love her? I love her better,
God forgive me, than anything in heaven or
earth."

Mrs. Pierce-Dawnay sat still in the
shadow. She gathered her mantle hastily
up over her shoulders again. She was
aware of a sudden chill.

"Jessie is a very fortunate girl," she
murmured.

Then she rose and began slowly putting
on her gloves.

"You will not go now, I imagine, Colonel
Enderby?" she inquired gently, and with,
perhaps, a faint spice of malice in her
tone.

"I don't know that," he answered; "I
cannot say yet. You have been wonderfully

good to me. But I must consider it all. It would be too hideous if she sacrificed herself through ignorance—through want of experience. I must wait; I must think it out."

Mrs. Pierce-Dawnay came a few steps nearer to him. She went on slowly buttoning her gloves. She did not look at Colonel Enderby, but there was a certain vibration in her voice as she spoke, which was curiously penetrating.

"See, I give you the chance of saving three persons from a possible catastrophe. Think twice before you let that chance slip through some quixotic half-morbid imagination about your own unworthiness. Things cannot go on as they are much longer up at the little red villa. Something will happen." She paused a moment. "I went into Jessie's room as I was going up to bed last night. She lay asleep, with her hands clasped under her pretty curly head. She was smiling, and her breath came as softly as a child's. I looked at her till—till all sorts of wild, wicked——"

"Hush, hush!" cried Philip, sternly. "There are things you may not say, and that I may not hear. There, sit down," he went on, more gently. "You don't quite know what you are saying; you are excited and ill. Let me go and call your maid to you."

"No, no," said Mrs. Pierce-Dawnay.

She sat down again in a purposeless sort of way. Her hands lay idly in her lap, and she gazed out at nothing, with dry, tired eyes. All her strength and courage had left her. She sat there in utter shame and weariness, while the sunshine slanted into the gay painted room, and the fountains splashed in the garden outside, and the palm leaves rattled together in the breeze, and the ring of voices and whir of the passing traffic sounded in from the narrow dusty street.

Galli, with his imperial head and pale, impassive face, came in softly to see if *monsieur* the colonel had finished his breakfast; but Philip motioned him impatiently away.

"Oh, I have sunk very low!" she almost moaned. "But you are strong and merciful, Colonel Enderby. If you knew what

I have suffered, you would not blame me very much."

"Who am I that I should dare blame you at all?" he asked quietly.

"I have borne it all so long; I have eaten my heart out with miserable thoughts," she went on, in the same dull nerveless way. "And I have had nobody to speak to, nobody to help me. Look, Colonel Enderby; I used to fancy myself born to console others, to reconstruct society, to bind up all broken hearts, to set the world straight. I have given up everything by degrees, all my foolish noble schemes, all my splendid dreams, everything. And what for? For a man who does not love me. I have neglected my old friends, forsaken my old pursuits and interests. He has laughed me out of all of them, with his gentle little mocking smile and his sweet voice."

"The scoundrel!" said Philip Enderby, under his breath.

"He has driven me into hardness, unbelief. He has even come between me and my husband's child, till the most terrible temptations have assailed me; till I have been on the edge of mortal sin. And yet I care for him," she added. "Heaven help me! I care for nothing else. What is this thing love, which men praise and belaud and represent as the glory and blossom of life? It seems to me a very curse and devil's gift. What does it do but wreck us, bewilder us, drive us crazy, poison all that is purest and best in us with one mad overmastering desire?"

Colonel Enderby shuddered. The words were terrible to him coming just at this moment. His own love was deep enough; but it was of a very different complexion. It made his brain giddy to look into the turgid depths of this woman's heart. Her entire disregard of conventionality, the singleness of her purpose, and the fierce sway of her passion, were revolting to him. He had no words to meet her with, no consolation to offer.

"Hadn't Jessie enough," she went on, looking up with a sudden flash of anger— "hadn't she enough, I say, with her radiant health and youth and beauty, with all the admiration society was ready to lavish upon

her, but she must have this man's love
also? Ah! those bright, innocent young
creatures are so cruel, so very cruel. Their
hands are never full enough; they clutch at
everything in their careless, light-hearted,
pitiless way. They leave nothing—nothing
for us older women. They won't allow us
the veriest pittance; they make us starve,
while they have sufficient to fill a multitude.
It is the old story of the rich man who,
with all his flocks and herds, must still have
his poor neighbour's one lamb. Hadn't she
enough already? Why couldn't she spare
me this man?"

"Does Jessie care for him?" interrupted
Philip, hoarsely.

"Pah! like that," Mrs. Pierce-Dawnay
answered. "As you care for the flower
you buy for fifty *centimes*, and let wither
for an hour in your button-hole! But remember," she added, standing up, and
speaking very clearly and distinctly—"remember, it is all my fault. I do not blame
her, and I have no right to blame him. I
thought she would amuse him. At first I
encouraged their being together. I only

thought of making the time pass pleasantly for him. Then, lastly, in a moment of insanity, I committed the unpardonable error of shutting them up together in the solitude of that hateful little villa. I have been a fool, and one pays pretty heavily for folly in this world.—Oh, take her, Colonel Enderby; for pity's sake, take her!"

She turned to him, laid her hand on his arm, and looked at him with eyes wild with entreaty.

"She likes you, and she is as charming as a summer's day. Take her, before—before——"

Eleanor's voice had risen almost into an inarticulate cry. There was a sound of footsteps on the loose gravel of the garden path just outside, and the window was suddenly darkened by an ample female figure. The Colonel and Mrs. Pierce-Dawnay turned hastily round, and moved a step or two apart.

"Oh, pardon me!" said Mrs. Murray, looking from one to the other with ill-concealed curiosity. "I am afraid I have interrupted you. I was told you were here,

Colonel Enderby. I was afraid of missing you. I thought I would just come, you know, and make sure. I did not know dear Mrs. Pierce-Dawnay was here too. This is an unexpected pleasure indeed."

Mrs. Murray was not quite a pleasant-looking old lady. Her eyes were small and twinkling; her red-brown hair—still suspiciously unfaded—was waved and puffed out over her ears. There was a disagreeably vivid colour upon her large cheeks and thin lips. She was extremely gracious and forthcoming; but one might detect a certain watchfulness and hardness behind her genial manner. Red Riding Hood's grandmother when she lay snugly in bed, with the white night-cap tied so neatly under the long lower jaw, making caressing speeches to that historic but unfortunate little maiden, must have looked a good deal as Mrs. Murray did at moments, I think.

Eleanor gathered herself together in an instant. She regained her usual fine manner, and looked very handsome, if a trifle fierce, as she bowed and slowly settled her mantle into its place, with sundry dainty pattings and smoothings. She was pale still, and the dark shade round her eyes had grown almost livid. But the elder lady's presence seemed to galvanize her into calm and self-control with remarkable promptitude.

"Now, I see I am in the way," Mrs. Murray continued. "Don't pray let me interrupt you. I should never forgive myself if I interrupted you."

"You don't interrupt us, believe me," responded Eleanor, with dangerous sweetness. "I was just going."

"Ah, now, I am distressed—really distressed!" cried the other lady, looking from one to the other with sharp, comprehensive glances; under which, it must be owned, Philip reddened slightly. "But I just looked in on my way to join Cecilia and our precious boy. I was passing, you see, and I should have so regretted missing Colonel Enderby altogether."

"I must go," said Eleanor. "Please call Parker, Colonel Enderby. You will find her waiting in the hall. I'll go down to the gate and stop the tram."

As she spoke, she swept out of the window, past Mrs. Murray, and into the glare of the hot sunny garden.

"Ah! my dear Mrs. Pierce-Dawnay," cried Mrs. Murray after her, "one moment. I have been so wishing to express our sense of your kindness in——"

But the lady addressed walked straight on, her head erect, her arms folded, her full crisp skirts dragging behind her over the path. Mrs. Murray's words died away; the geniality, too, died out of her countenance.

"Does the woman intend to be impertinent, I wonder?" she said, half aloud.

Colonel Enderby, followed by Parker, hurried across from the hotel after Mrs. Pierce-Dawnay to the gate. As he came up, she turned to him with a courageous smile. Philip could not help admiring her. There was something rather splendid about her, after all.

"Ah! there is the tram. How fortunate! Just at the right moment. Go and stop it, Parker."

Then she paused a moment, and looked steadily at the Colonel.

"You will not go to Spezia by the midday train?" she said, as she held out her hand to him.

Something of the honest sorrow and pity he felt for this unhappy woman got into Philip's blue eyes, as he answered—

"No; I remain here. I shall not go to Spezia."

"Thank you. God bless you!" said Eleanor, quickly.

There was a sob in her voice. She put up her hand and drew her veil down over her face, and then made him a charming little gesture of farewell, as she stepped up into the tramcar.

As Philip, revolving many things in his mind, walked slowly back from the gate, Mrs. Murray, stout, high-coloured, sharp-eyed, camp-stool in hand, met him.

"I really am annoyed at having intruded upon you," she said. "Had I known that you were engaged, of course I shouldn't have come. It was stupid of the hotel people not to tell me."

As she spoke, Mrs. Murray subjected Colonel Enderby to a minute and searching scrutiny. "Dear me, how he has improved!" she thought to herself. "And they say he has money. Can he be seriously occupied with that turbulent widow? Now, if Cecilia had only any spirit——" But Cecilia's fond parent was only too well aware that her daughter had the very smallest possible amount of spirit.

The Colonel was not disposed to be gracious.

"Pray don't apologize," he said stiffly. "Mrs. Pierce-Dawnay was just leaving."

He wanted immensely to get away and be alone; but with Mrs. Murray drawn up so squarely in front of him, it was not quite easy to manage.

"She is a remarkable-looking person," observed that lady, tentatively. "Of course, it is rather a delicate matter to touch upon, but it does seem a pity that she encourages my nephew so much, you know. It has alienated him from the rest of his family in a way we all regret, I can't deny that. Dear Bertie was always such a favourite."

Philip did not reply.

"In a large family like ours such things naturally are talked over, you know, Colonel Enderby. His relations see so little of him now. I have spoken my mind about it more than once. I was determined to come here and see for myself. Cecilia was rather unwilling, but I put it before her as a duty."

"Mrs. Farrell's obedience was always notable, I remember," observed Philip.

Mrs. Murray winced.

"Ah! poor dear Cecilia, how much she has gone through!" she exclaimed piously. "We act for the best. Sometimes I have reproached myself on her account."

Mrs. Murray gently shook her head and closed her eyes, as one whose thoughts lie far too deep for words. But the Colonel made no response; so Mrs. Murray re-opened her eyes after a few seconds, and returned from her abysmal depth of thought with a sort of jerk.

"I detain you," she said majestically.

"Well, I'm afraid I must go indoors, if you will excuse me," Philip assented. "I have to countermand some orders I gave last night."

The old lady's face became rapidly gracious again.

"You are not going, after all? Delightful!" she exclaimed, with a sharp little show of enthusiasm.

Colonel Enderby felt compelled to answer, though he did not the least enjoy submitting his actions for Mrs. Murray's approval.

"No, not for a few days yet;" and, lifting his hat, he passed into the house.

CHAPTER VII.

THE COLONEL CLASPS HANDS WITH HIS FATE.

On the eastern side of Genoa, but still within the limits of the city, there is a retired and unfrequented roadway. It offers a soothing contrast alike to the famous streets, with their long *façade* of splendid palaces and their swarming, hurrying, human crowds; and to those tortuous, narrow, melodramatic-looking by-lanes and passages which, with gloomy doorways opening out into dim dusky pavements, and heavily barred windows high up in the melancholy house-walls, form the less fashionable quarters of the brilliant city.—Murderous-looking places these last, where warm, robust, and ancient smells stagnate from year's end to year's end, and where you almost break your neck in the effort to catch a glimpse of the ribbon of radiant blue sky that palpitates between the contorted lines of the high, repellent house-roofs far above.

On one side, the roadway in question is bounded by a sea-wall, against which the waters of the Mediterranean gurgle and murmur hoarsely some fifteen feet below. On the other side are earthworks, overgrown with weeds and coarse grasses, in which shine the black burnished sides of cannon, their gloomy mouths pointing seaward. Beyond, the ground rises steeply in the picturesque garden of a charming villa, enclosed on the right by a high wall, masked with flowering creepers, and overtopped by the sombre spires of a row of cypresses. Looking westward, you command the vast semicircle of the Port, with its mass of shipping and glittering blue waters, framed in a broad crescent of stately painted houses, that rise up the sloping hillsides towards lustrous gardens and shimmering olive grounds,—guarded above by the purple steeps of the Apennines and by a ring of pale ghostly fortifications, outlined keen and clear against the sky.

About four o'clock in the afternoon following his critical conversation with Mrs. Pierce-Dawnay, Philip Enderby sauntered slowly up the roadway, absorbed by a multitude of pressing thoughts. He had come into Genoa on business. He had wandered rather aimlessly through the city, till he found himself landed in this comparatively retired spot.—It seemed a good place to rest in for a while, and try to arrive at conclusions.

Close by, on the left, where the earthworks ended, a quantity of shot was piled, each dark ball of metal giving off an iridescent dazzle of light as the sunshine touched it. A sentry, with his carbine on his shoulder, paced backwards and forwards, in front of the long, grey, windowless building of a powder-magazine. The man was a fine-looking fellow. His handsome southern face showed dark and ruddy above his blue-grey uniform and under his white linen-covered *képi;* and his white gaiters twinkled in the glaring sunlight as he moved.

The regular tramp of the sentry's feet and his tall, straight figure were very pleasant, somehow, to Colonel Enderby. He leaned back against the broad sea-wall, and proceeded to light a cigar in a leisurely and abstracted manner.

He wanted to be quite calm and judicial-minded, to go through the whole matter from beginning to end.—First, there was his love for Jessie. Philip did not waste much time on that point. In the last twenty-four hours it had become far too vital a part of him to need any questioning or careful scrutiny. Next, there was the question whether, under the circumstances, he was justified in declaring his love to her, in doing his utmost to win the young girl. Mrs. Pierce-Dawnay's wild words—some of them Philip tried to forget and put away from him; "The poor thing was half mad," he thought—had revealed to him a horrible and perilous condition of things at the Villa Mortelli. The pity and misery of the situation touched some of the deepest and finest chords in his nature. It was frightful to think of that fair, innocent child and the bitter war of conflicting feeling that was being waged round her all day long; frightful to think of her habitually breathing an atmosphere poisoned with the fumes of fruitless passion.

Philip thought and thought, weighed his own disabilities against the girl's danger; tried to look on into the future, and seize, by prophetic insight, an idea of how things would go—of married life for himself, and for Jessie; of the temptations, difficulties, that might arise and must be guarded against;—tried to get some notion of the whole new untried world of emotion and experience that lay before him;—counted, too, the risk of refusal. The disappointment would be terrible. Last night it seemed painful enough. What would it be if it came some weeks hence, when the sight of the girl's beauty and charm had become a habit and daily necessity?

The sentry paced on in the hot, still sunshine; the beautiful city lay glittering between the purple mountains and purple sea. Philip turned and looked away to the far southern horizon. He felt the critical moment had come—the moment of supreme decision, which would colour, for joy or sorrow, his whole future existence.

There were voices in the garden above; a sound of music from the open windows of the villa; a train of mules clattered by, with a jingling of bells about their fantastic harness; the sea swirled up over the points of rock, and splashed gently against the rough bases of the masonry; and the even tread of the soldier beat out through all the rest with an almost fateful ceaselessness and regularity.

Philip Enderby's whole spirit was shaken with unspoken prayer and strong immutable resolve. He was ready to take all risks. If God would give him the exquisite gift of this girl's love, he would dedicate himself henceforth to her service; he would keep himself pure and spotless for her sake; he would say no word, harbour no thought, that he need fear to tell her of. By tenderness, by constant care, by absolute devotion, he would make her happy. He would live for her, and her only.—" Ay, and die for her too, if that should seem best," he added suddenly, half aloud.

Then for a brief interval a great wave of sadness rushed over him, a swift dread of coming pain and disaster; but it passed as suddenly as it had come. And hope—hope of good things, of gracious, tender, and lovely things, ahead there in the coming days—was dominant in Colonel Enderby, as he made his way back through the Genoese streets that evening.

So, contrary perhaps to his better judgment, the Colonel gave way. Cynical persons will smile, and remind us that instances are but rare of successful resistance to a certain class of emotions. Worldly minded persons will complain that there is a savour of crudity and contemptible easiness in our hero's readiness to take a young lady so very obviously thrown at his head. For myself, I venture to hold my own opinions concerning my friend's conduct at this juncture, and to cry after him, as he goes away, filled with the joy of hope and promise,—Good luck to you, true heart! Heaven send you pleasant dreams and no rude awakening.

CHAPTER VIII.

ELEANOR TRIES TO BREAK HER CHAIN.

MEANWHILE, poor Mrs. Pierce-Dawnay had passed a sufficiently wretched day after her excited expedition of the morning. She had lain on her bed, half blinded with nervous headache, tired out, past caring whether her *démarche* had been a wise or a foolish one; only aware of active physical misery, as one long hour dragged by after another through the burning afternoon.

That worthy person, Parker, within whose flat, ungenerous-looking bosom beat a warm and faithful heart, shifted the pillows for her over and over again, and bathed the racked and throbbing head. Parker did not ask to have things explained to her. She entertained an unalterable conviction that the action of some man was at the bottom of every woman's troubles, and, on that basis, was invariably ready to build up a superstructure of practical help and tenderness. This stern hard-featured woman, notwithstanding her unresponsive face and didactic manner, was full of maternal instincts, which were wont to find their outward expression, silently but very soothingly, in the tending of her handsome, over-excitable mistress.

"You are the most solid comfort I have in life," the latter often said to her. "You are always there to fall back upon, and I cannot get along without some one to fall back upon."

Parker would reply with a sardonic smile. She did not always think her mistress very wise; but, possibly, she cared for her none the less on that account. Even the most devoted of lovers is sensible of a stirring of self-complacency in observing the aberrations of the beloved one's judgment. We must value ourselves above others for something, at times, or our own society would become intolerably tedious even to the most humble-minded of us, I fancy.

Nor had Jessie passed a day very much to her taste either. She had been alone; and to be alone was one of this young lady's severest trials. Mr. Ames had gone out, for him, quite early. She had only seen him at breakfast, when he had said very little, and stared at her once or twice with eyes as objectionably mournful as Malvolio's. Her step-mother had been invisible, and Parker had been invisible too—a fact which Jessie the less regretted, as she seldom found that good woman's society very enlivening. Little Miss Keat was in England. Colonel Enderby was gone.

Jessie wandered about disconsolately. Her trouble was, doubtless, of much the same order as that of a lively kitten, which can find nothing and nobody to play with, and which mews plaintively over the waste of its unemployed energies. Still, though the kitten's sense of discomfort may appear as a very trivial matter to some earnest soul toiling strenuously after a great and universal good, it is sufficiently trying and absorbing to the kitten itself, I imagine; the very limitations of its nature, which cause its discomforts to appear of so slight moment to the afore-mentioned earnest soul, necessarily making its small griefs the more urgent and the harder for the little creature to bear. We are too apt to forget that, though the troubles of deep and of shallow natures differ widely in kind, they do not differ, after all, very sensibly in degree. A tiny brook may be full to overflowing, as well as the mighty river that submerges a quarter of a continent.

Quite late that evening Eleanor came slowly downstairs. Her room had become unbearable. She threw a thin white woollen shawl about her head and shoulders, and, going out on to the terrace, sat down on the seat against the trellised arbour. The semi-darkness and cool, fragrant air of the night were grateful to her after those weary hours of feverish pain. She sat still, in a condition of mental vacuity, sensible only that she was physically less wretched than she had been, and that that in itself was an immeasurable boon.

At last the stillness was broken by the sound of a man's footsteps coming up the carriage drive. There was something light and yet leisurely in the tread which Eleanor immediately recognized. She remained perfectly quiet, hoping that Mr. Ames might go into the house without perceiving her presence. She dreaded meeting him after her late confession to Philip Enderby. She almost held her breath, and pressed herself back among the overhanging foliage of the arbour. She felt very weak and languid, wholly unfit for sustaining a part in a dialogue of an intimate and possibly painful character.

Bertie Ames paused for a moment. His eye had been caught by the faint, luminous glimmer of his cousin's white shawl. He came straight along the terrace, and stood a few paces from her.

"Is that you, Eleanor?" he inquired.

"Yes," she answered reluctantly.

It was too dark for either to see the other. Mrs. Pierce-Dawnay shifted her position slightly and sighed. She was frightened somehow. Presently Bertie spoke again.

"Colonel Enderby has not gone yet, I find. I had the privilege of seeing him for a few minutes this evening. I am not conceited enough to suppose that he wishes to pick a quarrel with me—I am not sufficiently important for that; but I must say his manner was hardly what I should define as conciliatory."

The young man waited after he had spoken. His silence seemed to compel an answer.

"I knew already that Colonel Enderby had decided to stay on a little longer," said Eleanor.

"So I supposed," observed Mr. Ames.

There was another silence.

"Bertie," Eleanor said at last, with a certain tremor in her voice, "would you mind very much going away for a week or so?"

"Thanks, cousin Nell," he replied. "I quite appreciate the excellence of your intentions in making that proposal. But

I don't think I quite see my way to leaving Terzia just now. There is my dear aunt, Mrs. Murray, for one thing, who has come here fired with all manner of philanthropic zeal to save me from dire dangers—so she intimates, at least. Then, you know, I don't much care about travelling without Antonio. I am horribly lazy about packing and so on, and I can't very well deprive you of your cook at a few hours' notice."

"I thought it would perhaps be better for every one," she said humbly. "I thought it might spare some pain."

Bertie laughed a little.

"Oh," he returned, with all possible sweetness, "as to that, we decided on the victim last night, Eleanor. Pray don't vex yourself about me. I assure you, I shall be quite interested in testing my powers of endurance. I have an enthusiasm for self-torture worthy of an Indian fakir just at the present moment."

Mrs. Pierce-Dawnay had risen hastily while he was speaking, and walked towards the house. In the doorway she turned round. The light from within fell on the young man's slim figure. She surveyed him critically from top to toe; there was a spice of contempt in the expression of her fine eyes.

"Yes, you are strikingly like an Indian fakir," she said. "You dress admirably for the part. There is a touch of exquisite realism, for instance, in that tuberose. You are like the fakir in this too—that you appear supremely indifferent to the fact that your experiments in self-torture may present an intensely disagreeable spectacle to other people."

Bertie Ames raised his eyebrows.

"Really," he said, "this demonstration appears to me a little uncalled for. You have got your own way in all essentials—as I predicted—won't that suffice?"

Then he took off his hat and gloves with much serenity and composure, and followed his cousin in a leisurely manner across the large flagged hall.

He found her with her head thrown back, leaning against the wall just at the foot of the staircase.

"Good heavens! Nell, what is the matter? You look as white as a sheet!" he cried.

Mrs. Pierce-Dawnay's lips were tremulous; she had a difficulty in speaking.

"It is very absurd, but I feel as if I couldn't get upstairs alone. I'm very sorry to trouble you, Bertie, but I am afraid I must ask you to go and call Parker for me."

Really it seemed a great pity that Mr. Ames had muddled his matrimonial prospects so hopelessly, for in many ways he would have made an admirable husband. He had all the instincts of a first-rate nurse; he was observant, endlessly patient, delightfully handy, and as quickly affected by the sight of physical suffering as the most soft-hearted of women.

"I can help you ten times better than Parker," he answered. "Here, let me come this side of you. Now take hold of the banisters with your other hand. Don't tumble over your gown. There!"

As he spoke he put his left arm firmly round Eleanor's waist, and carried rather than led her upstairs.

Half-way she paused to rest for a minute; she was faint and dizzy, and miserably weak. Whether she would or no, she leaned nearly her whole weight on the young man's encircling arm.

"Don't let us quarrel, Nell," he said, in a low voice. "We have never done that yet, you know. It would not be quite like us; it would give occasion to the enemy to blaspheme. Several people would look wise and say they had always foretold it, and rejoice with evil rejoicing if you and I were known to have fallen out. I am afraid I said some detestable things last night, but I believe I was in a condition of temporary insanity. A quarrel with you would be quite the most distressing thing that could befall me—now."

He emphasized the last word gently.

Eleanor fully realized the significance of that gentle emphasis. Still, his words had comfort in them of a kind; and she was in almost abject need of comfort at the moment.

"I am ready to go on, Bertie," she answered, very simply; "but I am so knocked up that if I talk I'm afraid I shall begin to cry."

At the stair-head Parker met them.

"I told you you weren't fit to go out, ma'am," she remarked, with some severity.

Even the kindest persons derive a certain pleasure from the fulfilment of their own dismal prophecies. It may be questioned whether Jeremiah would not have presented a much more lamentable figure to his contemporaries even than he did, if all his heart-breaking prognostications regarding coming captivity had proved, in the end, illusory.

Parker glanced at Mr. Ames with considerable dislike and suspicion.

"Mrs. Pierce-Dawnay is not going to sit up and talk to-night, sir," she said, with a sort of snap.

"Certainly not, my dear Mrs. Parker," replied that gentleman, with his most assuaging smile. "My cousin seems really ill. I have been out all day, you know, and I can't conceive what you have been doing to her meanwhile."

Parker sniffed. It was her way of expressing unlimited scorn and withering contempt for the frauds, prevarications, manners, morals, and general intelligence of the male sex.

CHAPTER IX.

"PEU DE GENS SAVENT ÊTRE VIEUX."

It is, perhaps, hardly necessary to state that Philip Enderby found Jessie more captivating than ever on his return to the little red villa. He had acquired, for a time at least, the right to think about her, to look at her, to admire her unrestrainedly. He had the right to let himself go—and, as most of us know, that sort of going is one of the very pleasantest sensations in the world. Then, Jessie was so frankly glad that he had returned, and she manifested the gladness after such a simple, radiant, dainty sort of fashion. She was, indeed, inimitably bright and fresh.

I fear that in speaking of this young lady I reiterate the above adjectives to the point of tediousness, and yet I cannot very well avoid it. Of some people it is enough to cover, or try to cover, the effect they produce on the mind of the spectator once and for all. It is not necessary to insist on the definition because there is a certain stability in the subject of it. But in the case of such persons as Jessie, and they are rare enough, the charm of whose charm consists in the fact that it is always new, always appealing with another touch of delicate originality, always shifting and changing, with a thousand fleeting lights and shadows —because there is an ephemeral quality about it, constant only in bewitching inconstancy—one is driven over and over again to note the sense of novelty, of refined surprise and quickened observation, that it produces upon the onlooker. Jessie, when pleased and desirous of pleasing, was undoubtedly a being created to be fallen in love with. Yes, notwithstanding his momentary misgivings and forecastings of possible tribulation, the Colonel was in an enviable situation at this moment. It would seem ridiculously superfluous to expend any of one's available stock of sympathy on him.

Mrs. Murray, though not exhibiting all the virtues supposed to be appropriate to the period of old age in their most patent and engaging form, is really a far more pathetic figure, to my thinking, than Philip Enderby, with his fine dash of heroism and poetic instinct.

She was not a nice old woman; and that in itself, rightly considered, is a terribly distressing thing. High-minded, pure-hearted persons need not be so very much commiserated after all, even if hard times do come to them now and again. They are secure of their reward somewhere—though not possibly in this present state of being—and that it will be a full and sufficient one we need not doubt. But as for narrow, shrewd, worldly souls, who have applied themselves diligently to scraping up all possible satisfactions off the surface of life, who are hopelessly rooted in the material order of things, whose hands are soiled with continual and eager grasping at vulgar transitory advantages,—these souls will doubtless have their reward too. But, good heavens! what a windy, stomach-achy sort of reward it promises to be! We will shed tears, bitter, yet proud, over our heroes, if you will; but, in pity's name, let us keep a few honest drops for the horrible disappointments of these poor, empty, starving wretches.

Mrs. Murray had, for many years, sedulously set herself to make a friend of the Mammon of Unrighteousness. But so far, I suppose, she had not been very successful in conciliating that popular deity, since she was still knocking about the world on a limited income, with no visible prospect of a speedy reception into everlasting or well-appointed habitations. She put an inordinate value on wealth, on social position, on the printing of names even in the second part of Dod's ten-and-sixpenny peerage. It seemed to her a very crown of blessing that people should have occasion to say of one: "Ah, dear Mrs. So-and-so, she was one of the Dashes, don't you know, and her mother was an Asterisk." Cecilia's marriage had been a very ripe and full-bodied glorification to her, because it introduced a sprig of nobility into the family. But now that poor Eugene had been gathered to his fathers, leaving his widow little enough beyond his debts, and that precious prefix to her name, Mrs. Murray began to think it was about time to look out for something solid in the way of yearly income. Cecilia, it was true, was sadly wanting in spirit: yet, as Mrs. Murray closed her thin red lips over her surprisingly white and even teeth, she flattered herself that very possibly she still had spirit enough for two.

From the moment she met Colonel Enderby on that critical Sunday evening she had planned a campaign. The check which she received from the news of his intended departure only served to stimulate her activity: we are all a trifle disposed to over-value the worth of a vanishing good. Now that she learnt he really proposed to stay on, the dear old lady set herself gallantly in battle array, beat the warlike drum, and played the inspiring fife in poor Cecilia's meek ears. Not loudly and openly, of course; but with innumerable hints, suggestions, touching reminiscences of early loves, and well-marshalled fears for poor darling little Johnnie, left, alas! so early without the healthy moral and social influences of a father's presence. All is fair, says the proverb, in love and in war; what, then, can possibly be unfair where love and war so obviously go along hand-in-hand?

"Johnnie is a high-spirited child, Cecilia," she said on one occasion, when, the high-spirited child having at last been consigned to his bed, the two ladies were spending the evening together in their little *salon*.

"Yes; I am always very thankful for it," answered Mrs. Farrell. "I think it shows he is healthy."

Mrs. Murray stuck her white bone needle into her strip of crochet, crossed her hands on what had formerly been her waist, and prepared for action. She was taking her ease in her inn, arrayed in a purple-and-black striped dressing-gown, and large, easy, red slippers. She had slumbered, too, a little after dinner—a habit that grows upon even the most vigilant of us with age— and her white lace cap had fetched way during the sweet abandonment of sleep, and inclined to the left in a somewhat lax and ill-regulated manner. But what did that matter? Even in undress uniform, Mrs. Murray felt equal to attacking and successfully routing her daughter.

"Of course, you can look at it in that way, Cecilia, if you like," she said sternly. "But it seems to me a great pity you should be so infatuated about the poor child; it can't be for his good. And it often obliges me to put things before you, and say things which I'd far rather not."

"Is anything the matter? Has Johnnie done wrong?" hastily inquired Mrs. Farrell.

"Ah! that's just like you, Cecilia—flaring up in a moment, before one has time to explain one's self. It is impossible ever to talk over anything quietly with you."

Mrs. Murray picked up her crochet and worked diligently for a minute or two. She knew her daughter as completely as a violinist knows his instrument. She had played on this poor human instrument often enough, and was accurately aware how to produce the effects she required.

Mrs. Farrell moved across and closed the door of communication between the *salon* and her bedroom. As she did so she paused for a few seconds to listen to the even breathing of her child.

"We might wake him," she observed parenthetically.

The elder lady worked on in silence.

"If you have anything to complain of in Johnnie's conduct, I should be so glad if you would tell me," resumed Mrs. Farrell. "I know how interested you are in him; I always value your advice."

"Nineteen, twenty, twenty-one," counted Mrs. Murray. "Yes; twenty—let me see—twenty—twenty-two. So you say, Cecilia; but, at the same time, I observe you generally resent my advice pretty hotly when I offer it to you. Twenty-three—twenty-four. Pray don't speak loud, my love; remember how wretchedly thin these foreign walls are."

Mrs. Farrell sat down wearily by the table. She was too much accustomed to sweeping accusations to resent them actively; but the anxious, harassed expression developed itself very sensibly in her worn and faded countenance.

"Twenty-eight," murmured Mrs. Murray. "You spoil Johnnie, and it makes me dreadfully nervous at times—nervous for you both. You have no head, you know, Cecilia; you never look forward. You merely think of gratifying the child in the passing moment. Ah! if poor Eugene had only been spared it would have been a great mercy for that boy!"

Cecilia bent down and plucked the little bits of fluff and dust off the tablecloth with trembling fingers.

"You used to say Eugene wouldn't make a good father," she said slowly, in a low voice.

"No, no, Cecilia; there you are entirely wrong," cried Mrs. Murray, with amazing energy. "You really have the most defective memory. I certainly never said that. It would have been the most unwarrantable thing to say; and I hope—I do hope—that I always weigh my words. I, at all events, recognized poor Eugene's good qualities. He was very fond of children —Eugene was very affectionate. A man is, almost invariably, more thoughtful for his child than for himself. I repeat, Eugene would have been the greatest blessing to that unfortunate boy."

Mrs. Murray picked up her crochet again.

"Thirty-one, thirty-two," she murmured, with dignity.

Upon my word, at times one is tempted to think these forbearing, long-suffering, humble-minded individuals will have a great deal to answer for some day. They give so much opportunity for sinning on the part of others. Whether the interests of public morality are, in any degree, served by this turning of the other cheek to the smiter is a question which will present itself to one now and again. It would have been far wholesomer for Mrs. Murray, surely, if her daughter had told her roundly that she was nothing better than an insolent old tyrant, and had then left her to digest in solitude that pungent truth. But Cecilia Farrell did nothing of the kind. She knew more was coming, and, with the patience of a Griselda, she waited for it.

"Johnnie wants a man," said Mrs.

Murray, after a while, in an oracular tone. "He needs a stronger hand than yours, Cecilia. I do my best; but then, who will listen to the advice of a poor, broken-down old woman like me?"

Mrs. Murray sighed and choked a little.

"I am sure, mother, I always try to do what you wish," murmured Cecilia, humbly.

"The Farrells are wild, all very wild," continued the old lady. "Johnnie takes after his father's family. He will give you a lot of trouble yet, my dear, and you're not equal to it. I am resolved to devote myself to you as long as I live. Whatever it costs me, I will never leave you. But who can tell? I am an old woman; I may be called away at a moment's notice, and then——"

Mrs. Farrell was quite moved. She got up, went to her mother's side, and bent down over her.

"You don't feel ill?" she said.

"Bless me! no, not in the least. Why do you ask, Cecilia, in that sudden sort of way? I'm not a bad colour am I? You don't see anything odd about my eyes?"

Being ill was the thing of all others she dreaded. Sudden death is useful to hoist up as a bogey for dramatic purposes: but at the slightest signs of approaching indisposition, the lady would have sent off post-haste for the nearest doctor. She recovered her composure, however, pretty promptly.

"I'm not ill now, but I may be any day. I lie awake at night, thinking of you and poor Johnnie. Ah! well——"

"Dear mother," said Mrs. Farrell, softly.

"Eugene was not a good husband to you, Cecilia." She glanced up at her daughter quickly. "Perhaps I once did you an injury; I have tried to repair it. I say to everybody, 'Cecilia and I are one; I will never leave her.' But seeing Colonel Enderby again has reminded me of many things."

Mrs. Farrell coloured. She stood awkwardly, in an uncertain lopsided way, by her mother's chair. "Cecilia's carriage always was wretchedly poor," thought Mrs. Murray.

"We won't talk of that, please"—Mrs.

Farrell spoke with a trace of hesitation—
"It was all over long ago."

"I am not so sure of that. You know I never push myself, Cecilia. I never ask for your confidence unless you offer it to me. I am very tenacious of appearing at all officious. I hope I am always delicate in these intimate matters. But I am not blind, you know; and I'm not at all so very sure that it was all over long ago."

Mrs. Murray closed her eyes and nodded her head emphatically, thereby causing her cap to lurch over a little further in the direction of her left ear.

"It seems to me that our meeting with Colonel Enderby was absolutely providential."

Then she applied herself diligently to counting her crochet again.

"I don't think I quite understand you, mother," remarked Cecilia, mildly, after a few moments' pause.

Mrs. Murray cleared her throat with a rasping noise. With all her devotion to her daughter's welfare, she was sorely tempted to box her ears soundly at times

However, she managed to dominate the liveliness of her irritation.

"You are too modest, Cecilia; you always undervalue yourself. Colonel Enderby was going. He met you in the garden next morning, and immediately decided to stay."

"Oh, it had nothing to do with me. He told me that he was going. It was after Mrs. Pierce-Dawnay's visit he changed his mind."

Mrs. Murray looked up sharply.

"Ah!" she said. She had received a check. "Mrs. Pierce-Dawnay is a bold, scheming woman," she broke out. "I haven't any too great opinion of her character. Colonel Enderby ought to be warned."

"Mother, do you think you had better interfere?" asked Mrs. Farrell, in a frightened voice.

"Four, five, six—slip one. How you do catch one up, Cecilia! Did I ever say I should interfere? But if a person of my age, and with my experience, may not sometimes try to keep a fellow-creature from making mistakes, it is hard. Poor Philip Enderby! Men never see through this sort of woman.—Ah, what a husband and father he would be! If I could see you married to Philip Enderby, I should, yes, I should—and poor little Johnnie too—I should die happy."

The excellent lady had become almost inarticulate. Her voice was broken; and two small tears essayed to make their downward way over the powdered surface of her cheeks. But they possessed no very large share of vitality, those two tears. They became confused amid an intricate system of but ill-concealed wrinkles, and, in fine, they never fell.

Cecilia was quite overcome by this exhibition of feeling. Still, her natural rectitude made her reply in a manner hardly calculated to soothe or satisfy her companion.

"Please don't be distressed, mother," she said; "but all that is quite out of the question."

She turned away. She was humble-minded enough, and to spare; yet there are certain admissions which no woman can make without a stab of pain, amounting to absolute anguish.

"You are too kind to see it; but I am old and plain now. No man will ever think of me in that way again."

Mrs. Murray rose.

"You are talking like a silly, sentimental schoolgirl of seventeen, instead of like a reasonable being of over forty. You know just as well as I do that a woman must meet a man half-way. Of course, if she stands up against the wall, and waits till he comes all of his own accord to ask her, she may stand up against the wall for ever. Love at first sight may be taught in boarding-schools, to keep little girls out of mischief; but it isn't taught anywhere else in the world as far as I know. Fiddle-de-dee!" cried Mrs. Murray, snapping her fingers fiercely; "do try to exercise a little common sense, instead of maundering about your age and your looks. You must make the best of yourself; you must be pleasant and seem anxious to please; you must flatter—delicately, of course; but still do it. They're all open to that. At bottom every man's as vain as a peacock. There are a hundred little things a woman can do. Well, then, do them. We must help ourselves, I tell you. You must come forward. A man at Colonel Enderby's age likes a woman who isn't too young. She is less flighty, she gives less trouble. Then, he has never married, so, of course, he has gone on caring for you. You have only got to play your cards well.—Yes, it is really providential," she added devoutly. " You must take more care of your dress—it's slovenly ; and buy some prettier boots in Genoa, with heels to them. And think of poor little Johnnie's future ! "

Ah ! what an inspiring and consolatory doctrine is that of the survival of the fittest. How agreeably it strengthens the hands of the capable, merciless strong, and causes the gentle and timid weak to duck under. How beautifully it is calculated to increase the exercise of the more robust virtues —pride, arrogance, cruelty, and such like. And what a very triumph of paradox, that eighteen centuries of Christianity should have evolved this gospel for us! However, fortunately or unfortunately, as you please, there lingers a leaven in human nature which prevents, as yet, its receiving this gospel in all its fulness. And those foolish persons—I count myself gladly among them —who have but a limited admiration for proud looks and high stomachs, will still cherish a hope of the survival of an unfit minority, among whom it may remain possible to cultivate gentleness, modesty, and a quiet love of personal liberty, without being immediately trampled underfoot.

But this is a digression: and a digression —in the estimation of persons living under the present system of express trains and postal telegrams, persons who have also, in the matter of amusement, a comprehensive habit of getting through as much in a week as would have lasted their forefathers a good twelvemonth—has a perilous affinity to the unpardonable sin. One trusts that here and there, in remote country districts, there may still be left a few kindly unenergetic folk, who cut out their lives by an older, more leisurely and stately pattern;

and who, instead of for ever calling out impatiently to a writer to stick to his text, are willing enough to wander down byways of thought, in comfortable, meditative fashion.

For myself, being naturally of an indolent and vagrant habit, I find it extremely difficult always to sit bolt upright on the coach-box and send my team at a spanking pace along the dusty high-road of my history, with an accurate remembrance of the stage just ahead, where I have to change horses, and set down or pick up another passenger. I have a weak, unworthy craving after rickety donkey-carts, and deep, high-banked country lanes, full of brambles and campion and calamint, that lead nowhere in particular: of old rut-tracks, across waste heaths and broad furze-dotted commons—dear, unfruitful places, with wide, still views of a monotonous and unhistoric description. And so, I pray kind heaven, that here and there I may have the good luck to meet with a reader of the old school, who will be ready enough to get down off the box-seat too, and, bestowing himself graciously in some humbler vehicle, dawdle with me a little by the way.

If a book tells a true story it can hardly fail to end but drearily. Why, then, should we hurry on so feverishly towards a foregone conclusion? Colonel Enderby is happy enough making love, after his quiet, reverent manner, at this moment; and bright-eyed, smiling Jessie is happy enough in receiving his homage. And if the other members of the company are rather on tenter-hooks meanwhile, I protest I don't care a rap. They were all pretty much the authors of their own discomforts, as far as I can see; and may, therefore, very justly suffer a little longer, while I take a stroll for a while and rest my wrists, which get tired and stiff enough with such long handling of the whip and the ribbons.

CHAPTER X.

MRS. MURRAY DECIDES TO PUT DOWN HER FOOT.

MRS. MURRAY, as the pleasant spring days slipped by, became increasingly convinced that it was her bounden duty to open Philip Enderby's eyes to what she was pleased to denote as—Mrs. Pierce-Dawnay's true character.

Like many persons whom it would be harsh to designate by the ill-sounding name of liar, Mrs. Murray had a very much more vivid sense of the importance of her own ends, than of the importance of strict veracity. The truth is big enough, after all, to take care of itself. What we poor mortals have to do is to take care ourselves. The fittest survive, no doubt—in the end the battle is to the strong; but even they have a pretty hard fight of it at times, and must struggle with a certain violence of determination for existence.

Perhaps Mrs. Murray underrated the strength of the enemy. That was excusable enough; many renowned commanders, both in ancient and modern history, have done the same. She had regarded Philip with a species of contempt, when, as a somewhat raw and inexperienced youth, he had first wooed Cecilia. Mrs. Murray was shrewd up to a certain point; beyond that point her cunning failed her; she was liable to fall into errors of judgment, and over-reach herself. It has been said that Satan himself is short-sighted. Not for an instant is it desired to imply a resemblance between a respectable old English lady of very fair social standing and the Prince of Darkness. Still, one may venture to admit the probability of a limitation in the acuteness of the supreme power of evil, since one recognizes such distinct limits in the case of those human beings who may be described as—not quite nice. Mrs. Murray could not shake off the impression that the Colonel was more or less of a silly fish.

He was in these days, no doubt, a fish extremely well worth angling for; but she fancied he would rise to an artificial fly of very common make. So the lady did not worry herself about refined arts and ingenious concealments of purpose. She waylaid Colonel Enderby at all available corners in the hotel; she planted her campstool solidly in front of him at all chance meetings out of doors. She praised her daughter; she mourned over her grandson; she bewailed that congenital tendency towards wildness on the part of the Farrells; she alluded touchingly to the past; she even went so far as to hint at a burdened conscience, and at a laudable desire for reparation.

"The man must be a fool or a flint if he doesn't give way," Mrs. Murray said to herself more than once; and the man, being neither fool nor flint, did give way in a degree. He was filled with a sincere commiseration for Mrs. Farrell, founded on an immense disgust for her mother.

The Colonel rarely permitted himself to say hard things, especially of a woman; but when, one morning, in the privacy of his own room, he found himself referring to Mrs. Murray as " an abominable, painted old harridan," his conscience did not accuse him of having committed a grave impropriety. In point of fact, he repeated the opprobrious epithet more than once, and found himself sensibly the better for so doing.

Still, Mrs. Murray could not flatter herself that her success was in proportion either to her wishes or her efforts. She saw so little of Colonel Enderby, after all. He was always up at the Villa Mortelli. One day she reached the point of exasperation: she decided to follow him up to the red villa, and fairly carry the war into the enemy's country.

The day in question was hot to the point of breathlessness. In the vain hope of getting a little air from the sea, the whole party sat out on the *loggia*, under a great red-and-drab striped awning, stretched from the house-wall above the window of the drawing-room; and forming a pretty effective shelter from the rays of the afternoon sun.

The land and sea reeled and danced in the palpitating heat mist.

Perhaps it was the heat, perhaps there was an intuitive sense of crossing intentions and desires among the little group of people assembled on the *loggia;* certainly the conversation had an inclination to run on dangerous topics. Eleanor was a trifle too vivid; Bertie a trifle too cynical; Cecilia Farrell even abnormally limp and harassed; Mrs. Murray distinctly acid under a fine assumption of geniality; the Colonel somewhat over-stiff and dignified.

Jessie, who at times appeared to possess a keenness of perception, hardly human, of coming storms, whether spiritual or physical, moved about restlessly. She had been arranging several great jars of flowers standing on a table within the open window of the drawing-room. Her charming figure had shown to great advantage as she stretched up to set the graceful flowering boughs in their place, and moved back a step or two to judge the general effect of her handiwork. Philip Enderby had sat and watched her. He found it a remarkably interesting occupation. Now she rested, just opposite to him, on the arm of one of the chairs on the *loggia*, idly twisting the sprigs of leaf and blossom that remained over into a dainty little wreath. Philip still watched her. Her small white hands, with their rounded, rosy finger-tips, were wonderfully pretty as she sorted and arranged the flowers.

"My dear Bertie," Mrs. Murray was saying, with an air which strove to be absolutely disengaged, "you are an authority in hotels and everything domestic. I want you to give darling Cecilia and me the benefit of your experience."

"I have never looked on hotels as exactly domestic institutions," returned Mr. Ames, in his soft rich voice. "But my experience is at everybody's service. It is briefly comprehended in one phrase—all hotels are more or less beastly, and all hotel-keepers are more or less swindlers. Does that help you much, dear aunt?"

Mrs. Murray indulged in a sharp-edged smile.

"You advise an apartment, then?" she said.

Colonel Enderby leant a little forward towards the girl.

"Who are you making that for?" he asked her.

She raised her eyes to his face with her usual bright, unshrinking gaze.

"Who? Oh, nobody, anybody—Bertie, Malvolio, you, if you like. I was really making it to please myself. I like to touch fresh leaves and flowers; they feel so nice. There, see!" and she laid the half-finished garland in his hand.

"I never advise anything," said Bertie Ames, with rather an unnecessary drawl. He stretched himself out lazily in his long cane chair, and repressed a yawn elaborately. "I always recommend people to do exactly what they want to do. Advice is a superfluity. Ninety-nine times out of a hundred people don't take it. The hundredth they do take it, with a reservation: then, of course, it turns out badly, and they think you an idiot, and never forgive you."

Mr. Ames looked fixedly at Mrs. Pierce-Dawnay as he spoke. She bent over a large piece of canvas, on which she was working a florid pattern in wools. That piece of canvas had become an institution; it had reappeared at intervals for some years, much to Jessie's irritation. Eleanor possessed but a limited capacity for small industries: her stitches had a curious habit of being crossed alternate ways, and at all conceivable angles. To Jessie, whose quick, concrete mind seized immediately on the right way of doing a thing, and whose deft fingers seemed incapable of an awkwardness, this bungling over needlework on the part of her step-mother was an incomprehensible stupidity.

As Mr. Ames spoke, Eleanor glanced up at him. Her forehead was contracted into a frown; but whether from a struggle to fathom the mysteries of cross-stitch or from some deeper anxiety, one could hardly pronounce.

"I don't think you're quite well, Bertie," she said suddenly. "Have you got neuralgia again?"

Mrs. Murray looked sharply from one of the speakers to the other. She had walked up from the tramcar, and it had been exceedingly warm. In proportion as elderly ladies patronize rouge and rice-powder, they should eschew physical exertion. Mrs. Murray's small eyes twinkled unpleasantly above her large, mottled cheeks.

"When I was a girl," she remarked, "young men of your age never complained of neuralgia."

"Probably not," Bertie answered slowly. "But, you see, when the members of the medical profession had stamped out all the fevers and small-pox, and so on, which persons of quality patronized in your youth, dear aunt, they then observed a probability of their speedily running short of patients altogether. So they immediately set to work, and discovered a number of nervous diseases—nice convenient things, which torture the surface of you, so to speak, and don't get near anything so vulgar as killing. Demand creates supply, and the power of faith is unlimited. As soon as we idle people were assured of the existence of nerves, we began to suffer from them. Nature has an endless power of adjusting herself. All things work together for good, as

Colonel Enderby would put it.—In this case, it was mainly for the good of the doctors, certainly. Do you follow me, dear aunt?"

Eleanor changed her position impatiently, with a kind of richly annoyed rustle.

"I really believe it would be cooler indoors," she said. "Jessie, will you go and play to us?"

The girl gathered up her flowers reluctantly.

"My neuralgia is of rather a peculiar kind," Bertie Ames went on calmly, turning to Philip Enderby, and addressing him with most disarming suavity. "It has proved baffling to many skilled physicians. I continue to suffer frightfully at times. My cousin really understands the case better than any one else, I believe. She is great on medical matters, you know; she studied them in connection with a scheme for reforming the unsanitary condition of many Turkish houses. She subscribed to an excellent little society—I wonder if you've any of the reports by you, Nell? they were delightful reading—a little society for sending out English ladies of middle age and unimpeachable morals to overhaul the harems. It was an understanding—I may mention, by the way—that the ladies selected should be distinctly plain. Altogether it was a remarkably interesting scheme. But somehow the Moslem husbands and fathers did not quite seem to see it. They—— "

Mrs. Pierce-Dawnay got up hastily.

"Bertie, you are absurd; you are intolerable!" she cried.

"Am I?" he inquired blandly. "I am so sorry. I was under the impression that I was agreeable. The conversation seemed to languish. I was merely doing my humble best to entertain your guests."

He rose slowly as he spoke.

"Shall I bring the sacred carpet indoors?" he added, pointing to Mrs. Pierce-Dawnay's somewhat colossal piece of needlework.

"Do as you like," she answered, with a touch of temper.

"I was just going to tell you, Colonel Enderby," Bertie resumed, with much composure, "when my cousin interrupted me, about my neuralgia. My cousin has been good enough to interest herself very much in the subject. We have talked it over a number of times—our quiet life here stimulates egotism, you know; it tempts one to be a little personal. We have arrived at the conclusion that the case is rather serious; that, in short, I suffer from neuralgia of the heart. It is a dangerous affection; it has been known, at times, partially to obscure the reason."

Colonel Enderby was standing up too. He looked full in the young man's handsome, brown eyes, as he answered—

"Upon my word, then, I should do my best to find a cure at once, if I were you. A man's life mayn't be worth very much; but as long as he does live, there can be no question as to the advantage of his keeping his reason."

"True," murmured Mr. Ames, with a slight lifting of the eyebrows. "Quite true, though just a shade brutal, perhaps, in the statement of it.—Yet, in some ways, it is singularly interesting to hear you say that. Now, Jessie, like a delightful little person, leave off weaving memorial garlands for me, or Malvolio, or Colonel Enderby, if he likes them—that was the phrase, I think?—and go and play to us. It appears to me we all require soothing."

Jessie turned from him with a slightly petulant gesture. Then she looked round at the rest of the company.

"You are really coming in?" she asked. "I don't like being alone. I play much better if I know people are listening."

"I am invariably ready to come and listen, Jessie," said Bertie, mildly.

"You are all very well," the girl answered, looking down and fingering her little wreath; "but you are not quite enough, Bertie, to be inspiring by yourself, you know."

"Oh, we'll all come!" cried Mrs. Pierce-Dawnay hastily. She moved a step or two aside with a sweep of full crisp skirts, and, turning to Mrs. Farrell, smiled and motioned her to pass in first at the open window.

Mrs. Murray essayed to rise; but her chair was low, and she was not always very agile in these days.

"Can I help you, mother?" asked Cecilia, coming towards her.

Mrs. Murray paused a moment before replying, then she said,—

"No, my dear; I think, on the whole, I'll remain where I am. You will excuse my not coming in with you?"

"Oh, most certainly! Pray don't move," responded Eleanor, with considerable alacrity.

"Colonel Enderby, you'll stay with me now, won't you?" Mrs. Murray went on. "I have not seen you these two days past, for more than a minute at a time. And there is nothing, if I may say so, which I enjoy more than a quiet chat with you. As one grows old, you know, one does so value good conversation. I have said to Cecilia more than once, 'Now, Colonel Enderby talks really well: none of that light, scrappy, senseless talk one hears so much of now; but real good conversation.' It reminds me of the sort of thing I was accustomed to years ago, in poor Mr. Murray's lifetime. We lived very much in political society then, you know. Ah, one so seldom meets a good talker nowadays!"

However admirable his speech might be, Philip could also command a convenient power of silence, when it suited him to do so. He bowed a speechless acknowledgment of his companion's polite observations. Her mature, not to say over-ripe, blandishments were eminently distasteful to him—all the more so just now, as he saw Mr. Ames within, in very close proximity to Jessie, opening the piano for her. Yet he could hardly desert Mrs. Murray after her late address. Philip's code of good manners demanded certain sacrifices of him; and he made them, as a rule, without flinching.

"I often think," said Mrs. Murray, in a low, confidential tone, shutting her eyes, raising her right hand, and then dropping it again with a little flop on her lap—"Yes, I often think to myself, Colonel Enderby, Ah! what a difference, when I see my own dear Cecilia and our hostess side by side! I observe people a great deal, you know. At my age what is there left for one to do but to observe, and strive to help a little now and then?"

Philip acquiesced silently again. What on earth could he say? The difference was sufficiently marked, and not the most courteous-minded of men could pretend it was very sensibly in poor Mrs. Farrell's favour.

"I know what every one would say," Mrs. Murray continued, with an air of remarkable candour. "Maternal prejudice, and all that sort of thing, you know, when I talk in this way. But I look below the surface, my dear Colonel; and the difference between those two women in heart, in temper, in feeling, in real devotion, is greater than any merely external differences."

Meanwhile, Jessie had begun playing. The girl usually selected somewhat dramatic and emotional music. Her taste was not by any means regulated, either in her choice of pieces or manner of rendering them, by the ordinary English-schoolroom standard. There was a dash of something audacious and professional in her style of playing, which had been known, before now, to excite not only surprise but alarm in the breasts of her auditors. Certain worthy ladies, for instance, who consecrated their superfluous energies to the cause of the German Jews, were little short of scandalized by Jessie's musical performances; and had left her step-mother's *appartement* in Florence, on more than one occasion, with their ears tingling, and an uncomfortable feeling that they had been assisting at something little short of an indecent orgy in the way of sound. I am not prepared to maintain that even Philip himself was not startled, at moments, by the unmistakable passion which this slender, dainty, innocent-eyed maiden contrived to throw into her playing. If he had heard any other girl play in that same broad, fearless fashion, he would have been disposed to call it the least bit unfeminine; but the Colonel's critical faculties were obscured where this individual girl was concerned. Jessie stood alone in his mind, and could no longer be subjected to the careful measuring meted out to other mortals. There is a love—a dear, old-fashioned, simple love, rarely enough found now, I fear, which swallowed the beloved object whole, so to speak—which ignored blemishes, overlooked defects, refused to admit the most patent of facts, if they threatened to detract in ever so slight a degree from the absolute perfection of the loved one. Philip's love was of this order—call it foolish, if you will, it is also, perhaps, very sadly beautiful.

Just as Mrs. Murray concluded her speech concerning the desirability of remembering that fair without is sometimes foul within, Jessie stopped playing abruptly. The air still vibrated with the storm of sound that had gone before. She turned and glanced round the room.

"Where is Colonel Enderby?" she asked, in her clear tones. "Didn't he come in?"

"He preferred the *loggia* and my dear aunt's society."

It was Bertie Ames who answered. Jessie opened her blue-grey eyes very wide.

Then, seeing Philip standing outside—"Colonel Enderby, do you really prefer it?" she cried, looking at him and smiling.

The rapidity with which Mrs. Murray

heaved herself up out of her low basket chair, and interposed her voluminous person between Philip and the open window, was positively astounding.

"Go on, go on, dear girl. We hear you charmingly out here. Delightful music; don't stop, pray," she said, waving her hand in an encouraging, yet imperative manner.

Bertie Ames laughed to himself. He leaned down above the girl's fair head and whispered—"When you are as old as my aunt, Mrs. Murray, will you know how to get your own way as well as she does?"

Jessie dashed her hands fiercely, at random, on the keyboard; her forehead was drawn into quite an angry frown.

"I hate that ill-conditioned old woman," she said, with her little white teeth set hard together. "And you bore me, Bertie, with your odious questions."

Mr. Ames leant his elbow on the top of the piano, and considered the girl thoughtfully for a minute or so. He had never seen her in quite this humour before, and it puzzled him.

"Dear me!" he murmured. "I wonder just how much that means."

As soon as Jessie was safely employed again, Mrs. Murray faced round upon Philip. There was a challenge in her bearing. She knew she had ventured pretty far.

"Now, my dear Colonel, we can go on with our talk in peace, I hope," she said.

But the Colonel, by this time, had thoroughly lost his temper. It seemed to him that Mrs. Murray had put herself outside the category of persons to whom one is bound to show respect and consideration. He had no intention of making a scene, but he was prepared to treat her with little mercy.

"Upon my word, Mrs. Murray," he replied, "I am not at all sure that I care to talk."

"No? Ah, well, then I will talk, and you shall listen," she said, still blocking the window with her large person.

Philip laughed. The impudence of this woman was astounding.

"Unfortunately, I am not inclined to listen either," he responded, looking her straight in the face, and slowly pulling the ends of his moustache.

Then that brave old lady, Mrs. Murray, showed the metal she was made of. She put her hand boldly through Philip Enderby's arm, and held him so.

"Oh! but you must listen, Colonel Enderby," she cried. "I have a dozen words I am bound to say to you. Come with me to the other end of the *loggia*."

To resist, to hang back under this employment of physical force, would have been ridiculous, unseemly, clearly undignified, and out of the question;—so he went.

Mrs. Murray took her amiable way to the back of the *loggia*, from whence a little flying iron staircase leads to the vineyard at the top of the cliff, behind the house. She leant up against the rusty railings of the staircase, which offered but a knife-edge of support to her broad back, and fanned herself with her pocket-handkerchief. Mrs. Murray felt it was a sadly common thing to do; but, poor soul, she was so painfully hot, what with one thing and another.

"My dear Colonel Enderby," she began,

in a wheedling tone, "I know you must think my behaviour most extraordinary."

Philip stood stiff, unresponsive, pre-eminently discouraging.

"Yes; most extraordinary. But then, you know, you cannot comprehend the feelings of a mother; no man can do that. We mothers are very lions when the happiness of our children is imperilled. My love for my darling, excellent, faithful Cecilia is my excuse. I cannot," cried Mrs. Murray, with fervour—"no, I cannot, Colonel Enderby, see you neglecting a golden opportunity, and rushing headlong into what I may call the very pit of destruction, knowing what I do know, knowing the contrast between these two women, without opening your eyes, without saying a warning word, without imploring you to——"

At the beginning of this impassioned address, Philip had simply stared; but, as the meaning of Mrs. Murray's words revealed itself, as he began to perceive what she was driving at, he gave a hasty ejaculation of repudiation and anger.

"No, no; I won't be interrupted!" she

cried, vehemently. "I can't stand by and see you giving way under the artful fascinations of this heartless woman—using that wretched little girl's prettiness, too, as a stalking-horse to compass her own bad ends—I can't stand by silent, when I know my own dearest child's welfare is at stake. That woman's desire for conquest is insatiable. I know her of old. She can't leave any man alone; she must have every one she meets dangling after her. Look at poor Bertie, estranged from his family, his prospects ruined, spending his money on her, keeping her servants, paying her bills! It makes me blush to see such folly!" she cried, overflowing with virtuous indignation. "And now you are to be ruined too. Why did she leave Florence, do you suppose? Simply, I tell you, because Florence had left her first. She'd filled her house with every sort and kind of riff-raff, socialists, mesmerists—heaven knows what. Poor Eugene Farrell was there nearly every night, at one time; with Cecilia at home, neglected and miserable, sitting up for him till I don't know what hour. Why did she come here to this dull little hole of a place? Because, I tell you, society would not countenance her goings-on any longer; because——"

Mrs. Murray stopped with a gasp: she was breathless. Nothing, indeed, short of physical incapacity would have stemmed the torrent of her eloquence at that moment.

Philip's righteous soul was full of wrath.

"Mrs. Murray," he said sternly, "I call it a vile and shameful thing to come to a woman's house, and then speak of her as you have just spoken of Mrs. Pierce-Dawnay. Fortunately, however, I do not believe what you say."

Mrs. Murray was somewhat cowed.

"Ah! but you are giving in to her," she said vindictively. "You are always here. You can't deny that; so, of course, it doesn't suit you to believe what I tell you about her."

"You are labouring under a complete misconception in this matter," the Colonel answered.

The position was odious to him, but he owed it to his hostess as well as to himself to be explicit.

"I have a great respect for Mrs. Pierce-Dawnay, but we are merely friends. She would be the first person to assure you of that fact."

Mrs. Murray looked up sharply. There was something in her companion's expression which left her in no doubt but that he was speaking the truth. The desire to know more was absolutely uncontrollable in her at that moment. Her eyes glistened with hard curiosity. She decided to stake her all.

"I am not so uncivil as to answer you as you answered me just now," she said, " and tell you roundly I don't believe you. I have my daughter's happiness at heart, Colonel Enderby. For her sake, poor dear child! I humble myself. A woman will put her pride in her pocket for love of her child. But just listen here. You were going away next day, when we met you that Sunday. Immediately after our meeting, you changed your mind suddenly. We have met frequently since. A certain construction may have been put upon your conduct, you know. For my daughter's sake, I have a right to ask—what made you stay, then Who did you stay for?"

Mrs. Murray folded her hands, and closed her thin red lips tightly. It was cleverly done, she felt, as she glanced at Philip. She had shifted the point of her attack in a masterly manner. Come what might, he could hardly refuse to answer her.

And Philip was not apt at evasions and subterfuges. Finding himself in an awkward place, he took the shortest and most direct way of getting out of it.

"I stayed," he replied, with quiet dignity, "because I am in love with Miss Pierce-Dawnay. I am about to ask her to be my wife."

For the life of her Mrs. Murray could not restrain a shrill cry. Then she burst out laughing. It was a very unpleasant, old, joyless sort of laugh.

"That little simpering slip of a schoolgirl!" she said. "Why, Philip Enderby, you are as great a simpleton as you were when I saw you first, five-and-twenty years ago!"

In a minute more she was standing before

her patient daughter, in the large, faded drawing-room. Her face looked very hard and old.

"Come, Cecilia," she said shortly, "we'll go back to the hotel. There may be letters waiting for us. Tea? No, thank you. I pay for my dinner at six o'clock, and I don't care to spoil it."

Mrs. Murray laughed again. One must allow, poor lady, that just then she appeared supremely unattractive.

BOOK FOURTH.
THE PROMISED LAND.

CHAPTER I.

QUESTION AND ANSWER.

As Philip Enderby stood there on the *loggia*, after Mrs. Murray had left him, he saw there was only one course open to him. She had forced his hand. He could finesse no longer, but must play his highest card at once. And yet he would have been very glad to wait a little, to make more sure, before he "put it to the proof, to win or lose it all." He hardly dared think what it would be to lose Jessie now! Mrs. Murray's parting words rang in his ears—though he hardly took them, perhaps, in the sense in which she had spoken them. The folly of his love lay, to him, not in the loving—that was natural enough—but rather in the hope of being loved in return.

Just then Jessie came to the window. She carried a large white straw hat in one hand, and her red umbrella in the other. The sun was getting low in the west. Its level rays streamed in under the coloured awning, and lighted up the slight form of the girl, as she stood, framed in the open window, with the background of the dim drawing-room behind her. Philip looked at her for a few seconds in silence. She was very young; she was almost startlingly pretty.

"It is impossible," he thought to himself. "She will refuse me, and then—well, men have had as sweet hopes knocked on the head before now, and will again, I suppose. Only I should have liked more time."

Jessie's face was not as placid as usual. Her mouth pouted a little, and there was a delicate line between her brown eyebrows.

"I think perhaps you did just as well to stay out here, Colonel Enderby," she said. "I played very badly."

She came on into the yellow glare of sunshine.

"Those people worry me, and Bertie says

inconvenient things. It is so easy to be pleasant and happy. I can't think why people need ever be anything else."

"Suppose," said the Colonel, gently, "we go away for a little while, and forget troublesome people and the inconvenient speeches. Will you come with me up the hill yonder, and see the sunset?"

He felt the words were not without a grain of feebleness; but it was difficult to be original at this juncture.

"Tell me first, before I settle whether I will go and look at the sunset or not, whether you really preferred staying out here with Mrs. Murray, to coming indoors with the rest of us?" the girl asked.

"I disliked immensely staying out here," Philip replied, with some warmth of feeling. "I stayed simply because I couldn't help myself."

Jessie's face brightened.

"Now we will go for our walk," she said. "I want to get out. I feel strange and restless; perhaps it will be nicer up there."

The little wood crowning the hill behind the Villa Mortelli, is a delectable place. It is thick with scrub-oak, ilex, and pine trees, rising among a tangled undergrowth of white heath and myrtle;—a quaint, suggestive little wood, fringed along the edge of it with grass and wild flowers, and possessing a number of narrow paths—crossed here and there with knotted roots, or soft with a brown layer of fir needles—which turn and twist, and wind in and out, till they make the small space seem quite vast and imposing.

The effective way of approaching this pleasant wilderness, is to pass along the level strip of vineyard above the house, to the left,—turn at right angles, under some old olive trees, up a narrow gully, where tall canes grow, and clatter their hard stems and long leaves together with a sharp, dry sound in the mountain breeze; pass the old reservoir, where the frogs keep up their discordant chatter; and then—crossing a space of coarse grass, dotted with clumps of heath, through which grey stone crops out here and there, to enter the wood from the rear.

A path leads on, right through it, to the

highest point of the hill, where stands a half circle of white marble benches—dilapidated things, upon which mosses have crept, and on which lichens have gathered, patched together with slabs and scraps of ancient carving, remnants probably of a Roman sarcophagus. This open space is shaded by some pines and a couple of oak trees, their trunks bent, and their branches cut over by the rush of the sea wind. It commands the same view as the villa below; but the expanse is wider, the horizon higher, the sense of freedom and solitude more complete.

As presiding genius of this sylvan retreat, some long-ago owner of the Villa Mortelli has been pleased to set up, on a tall carved pedestal, a marble image of Pan, with his broad chest, shaggy goat's legs, horns, and prick ears. But Pan, alas! has changed sadly since those far-off early days, when as a strange and awful presence—the godhead mysteriously joined to the brute beast—in the solemn twilight of summer mornings, he crossed the dewy Arcadian uplands, among the sleeping sheep-folds; or wandered from the mountain caverns and fragrant mountain marshes to the reed-beds, by the water-courses, in the fertile plain below; and brought good luck to the wild Arcadian hunters, and ravished the heart of Arcadian youth and maiden with the piercing sweetness of his oaten pipe. Yes; Pan has changed: and for the worse. Under the hand of the Italian artist, too often materializing what it touches, Pan has lost his godhead. Pan is chiefly beast now, or, at best, beast bound to a degraded manhood. He has looked on the lust of the flesh, and the pride of life—on the gorgeous corruption of Imperial and Papal Rome. He knows he is a creature of a monstrous birth, and the knowledge has made him foul.

While the sharp blue shadows of the oak leaves and fir needles played over his marble limbs, in the evening sunshine, there was something almost devilish about the image of Pan, keeping watch on the hilltop, above the little red villa. His wide, full lips parted in a wicked smile. There was an evil droop in his heavy eyelids, and a leer in the sightless eyes. The beating winter rains had left ugly stains and smirches upon him; and his pipes, and the hands which held them, were broken and defaced.

Philip Enderby and Jessie came up silently through the wood. The girl was still under the dominion of some unusual influence: she had not regained her ordinary gay, light-hearted bearing. And Philip was too fully possessed by the thought of the thing he must say to her, to have any small talk at command.

Jessie flung herself down on one of the moss grown benches, and pulled off her hat. She was strangely moved and excited.

"Oh, I am so tired of this place," she cried, looking away over the broad landscape. "It is always the same—except that sometimes it rains. Nothing ever happens; one day is just like another. And then I think of all the different countries I have never been to and the great cities, and all the beautiful, quick, vivid life that is going on elsewhere, where I cannot reach it, and I could cry with vexation and longing. Why does mamma keep me here like a bird in a cage—with that horrible old Mrs.

Murray, too, conning and staring at me through the wires!—and give me nothing to do but to hop up and down, and take my grain of seed and drop of water? I want to go away, away, away;—anywhere, everywhere;—see it, and know it all. You have moved about, you have wandered, don't you understand? I feel like the swallows in the spring-time, when they stretch out their long swift wings, and go northward. Oh, I am tired to death of this place! Why can't I leave it for ever?"

Philip straightened himself up. The crisis had come even sooner than he had expected it. This wild mood of Jessie's gave him a higher hope, a better opportunity, than he could have reckoned upon. Yet still it was difficult to speak. The might of his own emotion was almost terrible to him, as he looked at the lovely upturned face of the girl. Pure-lived men, when they give way to love, do it in a somewhat tremendous fashion. All the garnered strength of their manhood, unspent and unwasted, rushes forth in a flood of worship and desire.

"Jessie," he said at last, very gently;

"there is one way in which you may leave all this, that you are so tired of, behind you, and begin a new life."

Something in the tone of Colonel Enderby's voice arrested the girl's attention strongly. She rose up, tall and straight, in front of him, while the sunshine rested on her bright curly head; and looked deep into his blue eyes with a wondering, questioning expression.

"What way?" she asked.

"I am almost ashamed to tell you," he answered; "since you have so much to give, and I have so little to offer in return. I am as a very beggar before you. But there is only this one way in which I can help you. I love you, Jessie—love you with my whole soul. I lay my heart at your feet —take or leave it as you will, it must be yours always, just the same. But take it, darling," he said, "take it, and then come away with me as my wife."

The sun was sinking in a blaze of white light behind the far-off purple capes and headlands. The vineyards below lay already in dim shade; only the window of a high-standing painted villa, here and there, among the rich woods and gardens, caught the level rays on its rows of windows, and glared for a moment like a house of flame. The shadows lay long and dark across the turf, and under the trees; and the marble Pan leered from his pedestal, and smiled cruelly as he laid his curved lips to the holes in his broken pipe. Then the sun dropped suddenly; and the west grew pale, and the dim shade crept up quickly, stealthily, over the hillside and the trees; over the waiting lover and his mistress—while the limbs of the old pagan god seemed to gleam with a weird, unearthly light of their own, in the dusky wood behind them, now the kindly sun was gone.

"Jessie dearest, answer me," cried Philip Enderby, passionately. "Can you care for me? Can you trust me? Will you come?"

The girl turned her head for a moment, as the sunlight died, and the chill shadow came up over her. She gave a little shudder. Then she looked up at the Colonel.

"Yes," she answered softly; "I will come."

Philip took her two hands in his; and then stepped back, holding her at arm's length. He let his eyes rest steadily on her lovely face, on every line and curve of her graceful figure. He looked at his love long and carefully, and behold! she was very fair. His face grew pale. The strong man could have given way utterly at that moment, and sobbed aloud. It was too sweet, too wonderful. He felt as though his heart within him must break with love.

"Ah, God help me!" he said.

Yes, it is very awful, this desire of utter self-surrender, this wild worship, this madness of yearning towards the thing we love. It lies deeper than any mere gratification of the senses. Philosophers have called it hard names, and nearly split their brains over it, trying to solve the problem, trying to bridge the chasm, between the me and the not-me, the subject and the object, the noumenon and the phenomenon,—name it by what crack-jawed word you will. The struggle is old as existence. But the lover, of all men, dares attempt a solution most fateful and desperate when he thus casts his life down blindly at his mistress's feet.

For, alas! the chasm can never be bridged. The limits of our nature are set, and we can never cross them. Though lips press lips never so fondly, and hand clasp hand never so closely, and mind meet mind in the fullest illumination of friendship, there is still a measurable distance between us. Contact is not union, though men in all ages have striven to persuade themselves that it is. And hence comes the pain, the anguish, the exquisite bitterness of true love.

It was with some vague knowledge of all this that Philip Enderby looked at the girl before him.

But that long silent scrutiny and swift exclamation affected her painfully. Her charming face grew troubled, and the corners of her pretty mouth began to turn down and become ominously tremulous.

"Oh, what have we done?" she cried, trying to draw away her hands. "I am frightened."

Philip's expression changed. He grew

strong again; he was filled with a delicious right of protection.

"My darling," he answered, "there is nothing to be frightened at. You have done the sweetest and most gracious deed a woman can do. Only I love you too well, Jessie, and I don't know how to tell you about it. I would give my right hand to save you five minutes' sorrow or discomfort —and yet I frighten you. We men are awkward, lumbering, tongue-tied brutes at best, dear heart; we cannot express the tithe of what we feel."

Jessie looked hard at him for a minute or so, and then the most delightful smile began to dawn on her face.

"Do you really love me so very much?" she asked. "I believe it will all be very pleasant by-and-by, only I feel a little strange just at first. It seems so dreadfully serious. I do not like things to be too serious, you know."

She paused, and then came a little nearer to him. The colour deepened in her soft, cool cheeks; but she glanced up quite fearlessly into his face.

"Wouldn't you like to kiss me?" she said.

And Pan looked on. In the shadowy dusk a kiss was given and taken, as such kisses have been given and taken since the world began—as they will be given and taken, I suppose, till, innumerable ages hence, the drama of earthly existence is played out at last, and every created thing has passed back again into the impenetrable silence and mystery from out of which, at first, it came. But, for good or evil, two lives had bound themselves with one chain. A change had come over the night and the morning, and life could never be quite the same again.

Half an hour later, Jessie came quickly into the drawing-room of the Villa Mortelli. She walked directly up to her step-mother, and sat down by her. She laid her hand gently on Mrs. Pierce-Dawnay's, and nestled up to her side.

"Dear little Mamma," she said, "I am afraid I am very late."

There was something startling to Eleanor, both in the girl's action and in her address.

As a rule she avoided all caresses, and made no tender appeals of this kind to her stepmother's sympathy. Eleanor looked at her closely.

"Where have you been, my child?" she asked. "Are you tired?"

Colonel Enderby had followed the girl into the room.

"Jessie and I have been up the hill together, to look at the sunset," he said.

There was a certain resonance in his voice.

Eleanor, as she glanced at him, said to herself, "Why, he has changed; he is quite young. He is certainly a very distinguished-looking man."

Then she had a sudden perception of what had happened.

"Ah!" she cried, clasping her hands together, "you have spoken."

Philip threw back his head and smiled. There was wonderful light in his eyes.

"I am very happy," he said simply; "Jessie must tell you why."

The Colonel lingered late at the little red villa. The conversation was not very brilliant; and yet, perhaps, he found that evening one of the most delightful of his life. Jessie was quiet and subdued; she kept rather close to her step-mother: but the touch of shyness about her made her more bewitching than ever to her lover. She went down on to the terrace with him when he left at last; and there, in the fragrance and solemn stillness of the spring night, they parted. Philip Enderby had got very near the truth, after all, when he called himself happy.

CHAPTER II.

MRS. PIERCE-DAWNAY GROWS SUSPICIOUS OF HER HANDIWORK.

For some reason, Colonel Enderby had developed a strong dislike of Northern Italy, its hot, crowded, modern life, and haunting reminiscences of a not over pure-minded antiquity. A fit of home-sickness came upon him in the midst of his new-found happiness. Like the girl, he wanted to get away. He longed to carry off his charming bride as soon as might be; and her stepmother was not disposed to put any obstacle in the way of the fulfilment of his desires.

There are times when one has a right to be frankly egotistic, to be visibly and unblushingly absorbed in one's own small affairs. Jessie made the most of her privileges in this matter. She was warmly interested in the preparations for her wedding. Her soul was by no means too great to appreciate the fascinations of new dresses and millinery. She did not make any attempt to conceal her pleasure in receiving presents,—not intimating that diamonds are as dross when compared with the words of the lover who offers them. Every healthy-minded girl is a bit of a materialist, and possesses a very hearty respect for those more solid manifestations of affection sanctioned by society. Outward and visible signs are valuable as symbols of inward and spiritual graces in these as in more sacred matters; and, as a rule, are only despised by somewhat exaggerated and fantastical persons.

But Jessie's materialism—if it must needs be called by so ponderous a name—was far too graceful and delicate an affair in any way to disenchant her lover. It was the prettiest thing in the world to receive her thanks, to watch her sparkling pleasure at some fresh gift. Philip was touched and delighted by her endless power of enjoyment. He grew young in the light of her smiles and in the sound of her laughter. Early and late the thought of her possessed him.

Mr. Ames behaved very well during the time which elapsed between that memorable evening in the little wood behind the red villa and Jessie's wedding. He effaced himself. He paid frequent visits to friends in Genoa, and to Mrs. Murray, who, under the plea that the house Cecilia proposed taking at Tullingworth was not yet ready for her, lingered on still at Terzia. He really manifested most praiseworthy powers of endurance. Indeed, from the moment the engagement was publicly announced, he bore himself so bravely that Eleanor began to fancy she had over-estimated the strength of his feelings towards her step-daughter. And this fancy gave her new hope and courage. She threw herself enthusiastically into the situation; invited friends from Florence to be present at the wedding; lavishly expended both money and energy upon the girl's trousseau; and made arrangements with a somewhat regal munificence with the manager of one of the principal hotels in Genoa. For many reasons it seemed desirable that the wedding should not take place there in the country. The party from the Villa Mortelli would meet their guests in Genoa, the day before the wedding. Mrs. Pierce-Dawnay promised herself that it should be quite a brilliant little affair.

Everything, in short, seemed to be going off admirably, when an unexpected stumbling-block and rock of offence turned up in the shape of that devoted waiting-woman, Parker.

"I am sorry, ma'am," she said one evening, as she laid her mistress' dinner dress out on her bed, and pinched the lace ruffles in the sleeves of it into shape, "but I shan't be able to go with you on Tuesday. That new maid of Miss Jessie's can manage very well for you both for one night. I shall stay here till you come back."

Eleanor turned round upon her hastily.

"Really, Parker, at times you are extremely irritating. It isn't at all kind or nice of you to make difficulties just now. Why on earth can't you come?"

Parker stooped down, and arranged some

trimming on the front of the dress, which had got a trifle astray, with the utmost composure and precision.

"My feeling is against it, ma'am. There are things you know beforehand you'd better keep clear of, if you want to have your mind easy when you say your prayers of a night."

Mrs. Pierce-Dawnay flashed out angrily.

"Parker, you are simply insufferable! It's all very well to talk about an easy mind and so on; you are dreadfully jealous of Jessie's new maid. You want to make us all thoroughly uncomfortable, just because you fancy you are no longer absolutely indispensable."

"Very likely," replied Parker, grimly. "I suppose nobody cares much to see they can be done without. But I ain't going, all the same, ma'am, jealousy or no jealousy."

She knelt down before her mistress, and carefully put on the latter's neat evening shoes. In doing so she observed—

"It seems to me a fearful sort of thing, to give a mere child like her over to a man, to do what he likes with. I don't want to see her married, poor thing! no, nor him either. There's no saying where it'll all lead to for either of them. I don't object to a funeral, now. It's comfortable, in a way. You know it's all over and finished, and you can't be held accountable; but I don't care about the other."

Parker rose to her feet.

"You've a hair-pin coming out, ma'am—no, there near the top, to the left.—Not but what I think very well of Colonel Enderby, as men go," she added, rather inconsequently.

Parker, however, followed up her speech with a sniff, which seemed rather to neutralize the worth of this admission, and suggest that, in her opinion, even the best of men could not be expected to go very far.

Mr. Drake, too, sounded a somewhat discordant note more than once, in conversation with his friend. He had travelled back from Venice,—whither, after fruitless waiting for the Colonel at Spezia, he had betaken himself,—to act the part of best man at the coming ceremony. Mr. Drake was naturally gregarious. Under ordinary conditions, the society of some fifteen or twenty agreeable people, with an infinite capacity of talking well about nothing in particular, would have put him into high good-humour. But somehow, the presence of Mrs. Pierce-Dawnay's guests, gathered together in the large Genoese hotel, did not have a stimulating effect upon him. His native cheerfulness appeared to be in eclipse.

"It all seems so deucedly hurried, you know, Enderby," he said, when he got Philip alone for five minutes. "Of course, you know your own mind, and all that sort of thing, and I have no earthly business to offer an opinion on the subject. I know that. And, of course, she is tremendously pretty; she'll make an immense success in society at home.—Don't be angry, my dear fellow. If you will marry a young lady of a thousand, you must make up your mind to a little of that sort of thing. But all the same, I wish it hadn't been done like this, in a corner, as you may say. If your people had seen her, and so on, it would be different."

Then, as the Colonel began to manifest signs of impatience, not to say of anger, he cried out:—"There, there! I beg your pardon fifty times over, if I have annoyed you. Of course, it's all perfectly right. Only, upon my word——" Mr. Drake turned away and blew his nose energetically. "Confound it all," he said, "I am so awfully attached to you, Enderby, you know."

Eleanor was not in the habit of seeking private interviews with her step-daughter. She was very well aware that their relations were more satisfactory in public than under the expansive and intimate influences of a *tête-à-tête.* But on this last night, before handing her dead husband's child over into Philip Enderby's keeping, she had a strong necessity upon her to see and talk with the girl once more alone. The gentler instincts in Eleanor's strangely blended nature asserted themselves, and made her feel very tenderly towards Jessie at this particular moment. Then, too, the elder woman was not without a sense of her own short-comings. Everything was going well, surprisingly well; and yet she knew that she would be more comfortable, and that her conscience would more certainly acquit her of past errors, if cordial and affectionate words passed between her and her step-daughter on the eve of their parting.

She had bidden all her guests good-night, and it was growing late, when Mrs. Pierce-Dawnay walked up the long, bare, glaring passage of the Genoese hotel, and knocked softly at the girl's closed door. There was a pause before any response came from within. Eleanor had a sense of constraint, almost of timidity, as she waited.

The answer came at last, and she went in.

Jessie was standing in the middle of the room. She had taken off her gown; her arms were bare, and her curly hair hung in a luminous cloud about her charming face and shoulders. The room was encumbered with trunks and boxes, and with all that indescribable litter which goes with a great and important packing. Spread out over an armchair, in one corner, lay the rich, soft folds of the girl's white wedding dress, which she had been trying on earlier in the evening. The night was warm, and one of the tall, muslin-curtained windows stood ajar, behind the wooden lattice of the closed shutters, letting in a thick, continuous hum of voices and patter of footsteps from the great *piazza* below. Genoa was still awake, and moving restlessly about her wide squares and streets of palaces.

Eleanor's dramatic instinct was strong. The sight of this solitary girlish figure, in the high quiet room, with the signs of her marriage and coming departure about her, and the urgent stir and hot full life of the great city surging in through the open window, affected her powerfully. She forgot all the differences which had arisen between them—all those crossings of interest which had put them into an attitude of such disastrous antagonism—and simply yearned, in wholesome womanly love and kindliness, towards this fair young creature, setting forth so gaily on the perilous voyage of matrimony.

"Jessie, dearest child," she said, "I felt I could not go to bed to-night without coming to look at you once more."

She took the girl's hand in both hers and made her turn round, so that the light of the gas-jet, above the marble-topped toilette-table, might fall on her face. Then she drew the girl close to her, and kissed her rounded cheek.

"You look very sweet," she said. "See, dear child," she went on earnestly, "I want you truly and honestly to answer me one question. You are on the eve of a great undertaking,—of, perhaps, the most important event that can happen in a woman's life. Tell me, Jessie, are you quite sure you are happy?"

The girl moved a step away, and looked back at her step-mother unshrinkingly. There was no hint of trouble or misgiving in her pretty eyes.

"Ah, that is so like you, little Mamma," she said, smiling. "You are so fond of assurances. Certainly, I am quite happy. Why should I be anything else? I am immensely interested. I find it all delightful."

The words might have carried conviction, surely, to her listener; but Eleanor wanted more. She felt, as she had often felt before now, that there was something baffling, something curiously difficult to grasp, in this brilliant being's personality. At times, she had asked herself whether her step-daughter was the most absolutely natural, or the most consummately artificial woman she had ever met with.

"But tell me, Jessie," she insisted, "don't mind telling me—remember, I have been a girl too, and can enter into your thoughts and feelings; surely we may speak freely to each other just now, if we may ever speak freely at all—are you sure you are really in love with Colonel Enderby?"

The girl's face grew graver.

"I never quite understand what people mean when they say all those things about being in love," she answered. "They seem to imply that it is a mysterious and extraordinary condition. I never have understood, and I do not want to do so. It sounds rather uncomfortable and crazy. But I like him very much; I like being with him. He is very pleasant; he is beautifully kind to me."

She smiled, and drew away her hand,

which Eleanor was still holding, with an apologetic little shiver.

"Pardon me, but your hands are so very cold, little Mamma," she said; and then added, after a moment's reflection, "I don't quite see why you should ask me these questions to-night. I took for granted you were satisfied, and had meant it all to happen so from the first."

Jessie spoke with perfect openness and good-temper, as though making the most obvious of statements. But to Eleanor the words came as a violent shock. It is not a little disconcerting to hear something which you have known, yet tried not to know,—not acknowledged even in secret to yourself,—proclaimed clearly, concisely, and without the smallest hint of confusion by another person.

Mrs. Pierce-Dawnay stood for a moment uncertain what to do, how to answer. She had an unreasoning revulsion of sentiment against this marriage of her own making—a revulsion against poor Jessie, too. She was addicted to prompt and daring action; to slightly desperate efforts at making the crooked straight, and rough places plain; but in this case, desire it how she might, prompt and daring action was out of the question. The whole matter had got beyond her control. There lay Jessie's wedding dress; there were her trunks, ready strapped and labelled; there, on the toilette-table, gleamed the string of pearls her lover had given her to wear to-morrow. In the face of these plain, tangible tokens of the position, Eleanor saw she was powerless. Too, her feeling of alarm was, after all, but transitory. She recalled Colonel Enderby's looks when he had bidden her good-night an hour before. They were certainly those of a man who is sufficiently confident of the good promise of his prospects.

"I am attaching an exaggerated importance to Jessie's words," she thought. "Putting a false construction on them, perhaps. I always read between the lines too cleverly, and worry myself when there is no real cause for it."

The girl, meanwhile, had turned back to the looking-glass, and was engaged in coiling up her bright hair.

"I am getting so tired, little Mamma," she said, in a plaintive voice.

The remark brought Eleanor to a quick decision. She determined, in any case, to speak a good word for Philip Enderby before she took leave of her step-daughter.

"I won't keep you any longer, dear child," she said. "Sleep well, and look your prettiest to-morrow. Only remember, Jessie, Colonel Enderby loves you passionately— more deeply than you can measure. Don't disappoint him; don't undervalue his love. Such affection is a great possession to any woman; but it is sensitive, it is easily wounded. Be careful, dear. You will try to please him always, and be a devoted wife to him, won't you?"

The girl passed her hand across her smooth forehead rather wearily.

"Oh yes, of course I shall, Mamma. It would be horribly stupid to do anything else."

And with this somewhat enigmatic reply, Eleanor had to content herself.

CHAPTER III.

IN WHICH MALVOLIO DOES THE HONOURS OF THE VILLA MORTELLI.

Fortunately, the misanthropic views on the subject of marriage expressed by Parker do not obtain at all universally. Quite a large gathering waited in the handsome black and white English church in the Via Goito next forenoon. Most weddings are interesting, and this particular wedding was uncommonly so. It had a halo of romance hanging about it, a savour of the unexpected and improbable. The bride was so young and so ravishingly pretty. The bridegroom, on the other hand, was not at all young; but he was somebody, he had made a name for himself, he dressed well, he looked an eminent gentleman.

People smiled and gossiped good-humouredly.—" Yes, it was romantic. Did she

have her gown made here or in Paris?
Paris, probably. It fitted miraculously, but
it was a little pinched in the trimmings.
The pearls were good; and how well they
looked against her fair skin—just that
warm suggestion of tone in it which is so
lovely. Ah!—like that,—everybody hoped
all would go well with them, and wondered
—for the step-mother was incontestably a
very striking person—wondered whether
there might not be just a little something
behind, an explanation, you know, a *dessous-des-cartes?*"

Colonel Enderby was impatient to hurry
his bride away, when she came down after
the breakfast, dressed for her journey. He
turned restive under all this ceremonial and
publicity. The staring, the talking, the
small compliments that had to be amiably
responded to, the general sense of being
the hero of a highly amusing and popular
comedy, was anything but agreeable to him.
The Colonel was both modest and proud.
He bore himself extremely well; but he did
not in the least wish to extend the period
of his ordeal.

"We won't miss our train," he said at last to Jessie, as she stood in the centre of a little circle of friends, in the frescoed *salon* of the hotel.

Certainly the young lady repaid inspection wonderfully well at that moment. The touch of demureness in her delicate grey travelling gown and grey bonnet, and a little assumption of dignity in her manner, only brought her almost infantine prettiness into more telling relief. To Philip Enderby she was wholly adorable, standing there fastening her long gloves, and smiling at the assembled company. As a necessary consequence of that adoration he had the very liveliest longing to get her away from all these people. It seemed to him little short of profanation that any one but himself should venture to gaze at her.

"Yes, it is getting late. You had certainly better start," drawled Bertie Ames.

He moved away, and took up his position by the door of the *salon* as he spoke.

"It would be rather unlucky to begin so immediately by losing something, you know—even if it was only the train to

Milan. The losing can very well keep till later."

Jessie went through the inevitable hand-shaking and embracing with calmness and resignation. She paused a moment opposite to her step-mother.

"Good-bye, dear little Mamma, till we meet in England, delightful England," she said brightly.

Then the two women kissed each other.

Tears were in Eleanor's eyes as she pressed Colonel Enderby's hand in hers.

"Ah, my good friend," she said, "I pray God you may be very happy."

Her expression was appealing, and there was a fine intensity in it.

"I am very happy," he replied quietly, as he bowed over her clasped hands; "and I am grateful to you."

"Thank you for that."

"You need not fear but that I shall guard the treasure you have given me very jealously.—You know, you have only to command me at any time, if I can serve you."

Eleanor made a rapid gesture of assent.

She felt an immense honour and regard for this man.

Bertie stood by the door, waiting for Jessie to pass out into the great hall beyond. He looked very languid, very gentleman-like, and wore the inevitable gardenia, along with the orange blossom, in the button-hole of his frock coat. As the young lady approached him, a singular thinness and pallor came over his dark face.

"I shall miss my charming little cousin a good deal," he said, taking her hand in his for a moment. "Farewell, Jessie Enderby."

The girl started visibly at the sound of her new name. She gave herself a curious little shake.

"I am glad you will miss me," she answered. Then, glancing up at him quickly, "But you will soon console yourself, Bertie. It will pass; as for that, one does not miss any one very long."

Bertie Ames put up his eyebrows and shrugged his shoulders.

"You are admirably philosophic under all

circumstances, Jessie. Yes, decidedly I will do my best to find consolations."

Colonel Enderby, escaping from the affectionate overflowings of Mr. Drake, arrived just in time to hear Bertie's last words. The two men exchanged a not altogether friendly glance, and merely bowed to each other.

Outside in the hall, Jessie turned suddenly to her husband. She passed her hand through his arm, and clung to him with a strange vehemence.

"Philip, will you promise always to be as kind to me as you are now?" she cried.

"My darling," he exclaimed, "what a question!"

He was half pleased, half pained by the girl's earnestness.

"God forbid that you should ever find me one whit less kind. I am not much given to changing, Jessie. I must always love you better, hold you dearer, than life itself."

Philip Enderby's expression was very tender and pathetic as he looked at her.

A little crowd of friends, backed by all

the *employés* of the hotel—who could not forbear making the most of this opportunity of sight-seeing and gossip—thronged into the hall after them. Jessie recovered herself quickly. She had an innate regard for appearances. She passed out to the carriage, brilliant, smiling, and apparently light-hearted as usual.

"*Mon Dieu*," whispered a French chambermaid to the *garçon* near her; "but how young she is, and how pretty! Wait a little, there will be three to the *ménage* one of these days."

Her companion smiled blandly, spread out his hands with an air of wide and varied experience, and replied—

"Ah, one cannot foretell. They are English. The habits of the English are extremely droll."

The hall of the hotel was destined to witness another episode, of a somewhat penetrating character, before the close of Colonel Enderby's wedding day.

Eleanor had arranged to set out on her drive back to the Villa Mortelli about half-past five o'clock. By that time her guests would have gone their several ways; and the traffic on the Corniche road would be less heavy in the evening. A little before the half-hour she came downstairs. The glory of the day was over, and Eleanor had exchanged her wedding finery for one of her ordinary black dresses, with its many crisp pleatings and flouncings. Over it she wore a long, light-coloured coat, to preserve her clothes from the dusty horrors of the high-road.

The excitement, not only of this day, but of the several months, had come to an abrupt termination, and with Eleanor the reaction was already setting in. Her plans had prospered; everything had worked perfectly; she could assure herself, almost without a misgiving, that she had done the best for everybody—for Jessie, for Colonel Enderby, and for Bertie Ames too, in the long run, though at present he might be a trifle slow to acknowledge it: people are so ridiculously blind at times to their own highest good! For herself, she had brought a relation of a difficult and perplexing nature to a happy close; she had extricated herself from a situation which had threatened to become actually tragic. On the face of it, she had every reason for self-congratulation just now. She should have folded her hands restfully, thanked a benignant Providence for past favours, and looked towards the future with confidence and serenity. But in point of fact she did none of these comfortable things, as she came slowly downstairs into the great cool hall,—with its plants and palms in green wooden boxes, and its small army of smiling porters and waiters, lounging about, and staring good-humouredly at the stream of people crossing and recrossing each other on the pavement outside, and at the crowded movement of the broad, sun-blinded square beyond.

Eleanor was tried and worried. She was singularly incapable in the small affairs of daily life. She had been obliged to pack her own trunk and valise—Jessie's maid having departed along with her mistress—and this simple business had caused her considerable embarrassment. She felt cross with Parker; injured at her desertion. And then, too, she had never contemplated this dull, uninteresting space of time, when the old excitement would be over, and no new one would have appeared to take its place.

To do Eleanor justice, I must insist upon the fact that she had looked no further, planned for nothing, beyond Jessie's marriage. That had presented itself to her as the end to be attained, as the supreme solution of all alarms and difficulties. What might happen later, she had but very vaguely imagined. All must then go well, she supposed; but she had shrunk with a creditable instinct from exploring the probabilities of the future, even in thought. It was the nature of the woman to fling herself, with almost hysterical vehemence, in pursuit of a definite object; disregarding consequences, disregarding side issues, with a childish inconsequence. Now, her object being attained, she found herself suddenly face to face with that enigmatical future; and at a moment, too, when she felt particularly ordinary, commonplace, and acutely disturbed by the vulgar details of existence.

A sense of uneasiness and disquiet laid hold on Mrs. Pierce-Dawnay as she waited for her carriage. She looked out at the bright, dusty, picturesque *piazza* for a minute or so, and then turned and glanced towards the door of the smoking-room, in the corridor on the right, from whence she expected Bertie every moment to come and join her. She hated delay. She bit her lip and patted her neatly shod foot on the marble floor with growing impatience.

The hotel manager, a rotund, middle-aged Italian, blessed with a sleek white face, closely cropped black hair, and an air of indescribable benevolence, came forward, rubbing his fat hands, and bowing profusely.

"He regretted immensely that madame should be kept waiting, but it still wanted some minutes to the hour she had named in her esteemed command for the carriage. He could never sufficiently express his gratitude to madame for her goodness in having selected his hotel as a suitable locality where might be accomplished the interesting event of the morning. Ah! and by the way, Mr. Ames,—the gentleman who had left by the half-past four o'clock train,—had entrusted him with a letter for madame, which he now did himself the honour to present to her. On receiving it he had proposed to permit no delay, to deliver it to her immediately; but the gentleman had instructed him to wait till madame was leaving."

Eleanor grew nearly as white as the marble quarries under her feet, as she took the note that the beaming Italian held out to her. A great horror came over her, a sudden frightful self-revelation. But she mastered herself. She thanked the florid-mannered manager for his courtesy. The arrangements had been admirable in every particular; they left nothing to be desired.

The man laid one thick white hand upon his wilderness of shirt-bosom, and bowed with speechless fervour.

"Ah! but there was the carriage at last, as madame, no doubt, perceived. In three seconds her baggage would be placed—so. Now might he have the honour of assisting her to enter it?"

She walked out to the carriage firmly,

and even contrived to make one or two suitable little speeches to the engaging Italian by the way — which, under the circumstances, was little short of heroic. But her heart was like a stone. She had no need to read Bertie Ames' letter—she knew quite well what was in it already.

Mrs. Pierce-Dawnay drove through the magnificent Genoese streets, with their solemn splendour of building, and their teeming, restless, charming, grotesque human figures; through the long, arid, straggling suburbs, beyond the fortifications; and out on to the dusty high-road, sitting stiff and upright in the carriage, while the yellow evening sunshine poured down upon and scorched her. The great blue rollers rushed joyously up against the sea-wall on the left, behind the tall narrow warehouses and flat market-gardens, and broke in clouds of snowy foam with a deep-mouthed roar, which might be heard above all the braying of mules, and shouting and swearing of savage-looking drivers, and rattle of wheels, and grate of tramcars on the high-road. Dusty roses hung over the high walls on the right, and richly coloured villas glowed amid the cool glossy green of their old walled gardens. Now and again there was a block of waggons or mule trains, and the carriage drew up for a while in the midst of a struggling, seething mass of straining animals and yelling, lashing human beings.

Ordinarily, Eleanor would have been exceedingly well aware both of the beautiful and of the repulsive elements in her surroundings; but, as it was, she saw and heeded nothing. She had glanced at the first few lines of Bertie's farewell letter, and a shame, a self-contempt, so scathing had overtaken her that the drama of sea and sky and sunset, of the contrast between the dignity and the brutality of the scene before her, was thin and insignificant compared with the depth of her own emotion.

"Good-byes are unpleasant things," wrote Bertie Ames. "We have had plenty of them already to-day; so, dear Cousin, I venture to spare myself the pain of saying that odious word to you. Of course, I don't for an instant permit myself the impertinence of supposing you contemplated my remaining your guest after to-day. Jessie's presence satisfied *les convenances.* You are too kind to give me my *congé,* but I understand——"

Eleanor read no further. Mistaken, exaggerated, imprudent, even at moments cruel, as she was, the springs of womanly modesty still rose pure and unpolluted within her. She recoiled with passionate disgust and horror. Good heavens! that a man should ever have cause to say such things to her! that she should have been so utterly blind and stupid, in her mad desire to clear the way, to get rid of the obstacle that seemed to interpose between herself and the thing she longed after—as to have ignored the obvious result, and so checkmated herself. She had been too hot-headed, she had played too high, and lost everything, including her own self-respect. And then, in an agony of terror, she began to ask herself whether she might not have compassed the ruin of other lives besides her own?

The only safe thing, after all, is to leave events in the hands of Fate or Providence—

say which you will. Directly petty human purpose comes in, trying to modify, or wrest to its own uses, the actions of others, so soon does Nemesis rise up, and follow on after us,—on, on, with ever-nearing footsteps, till the sound of her terrible tread is in our ears, and we feel the awful gloom of her approaching presence. But she may pass us by?—Oh yes; pass us, the sinners, leave us in peace and comfort; pass us to crush, to maim, to mutilate those whom we used so thoughtlessly as tools and puppets. It is easy enough to set the machine of destiny in motion, but once the great wheels are whirring, turning, spinning, no mortal hand is strong enough to stay them again.

The dusk had fallen when the carriage drew up at the front door of the Villa Mortelli. The house looked grim and deserted. A dull light was burning in the bare, cold hall. The driver pulled the bell and drummed on the panels of the half-open door; but the noise he made evoked nothing more substantial than a dreary echo.

Utterly weary and self-abased, Mrs. Pierce-Dawnay got out of the carriage, and went indoors. In the dimness of the hall, she could perceive but one living creature, one being there ready to welcome her home.

On the low marble pillar, ending the balusters at the bottom of the staircase, sat Malvolio, hunched up together, his wizened face more wrinkled, anxious, mournful than ever. As Eleanor came in at the door, he craned out his skinny neck, peeping and peering into the darkness behind her, with quick uneasy liftings of the eyelids and eyebrows. He had on the little red tattered jacket in which Bertie sometimes clothed him in cold or rainy weather; while, on the narrow bosom of it, Antonio, with a truly Italian taste for staring incongruities, had pinned a large bunch of orange blossom, tied with a flaring bow of white satin ribbon. When the monkey's quick instinct assured him that his master had not come home too, he turned fiercely on Eleanor, pointing, grinning, chattering at her with impotent malignity. There was a diabolical light in the creature's sad eyes, and something absolutely hideous in its furious gestures.

Eleanor, overstrung and exhausted, could

not bear it. She called aloud in terror and agitation; and her voice rang up the cold, white staircase, and through the empty, silent rooms of the little red villa.

"They are all, all gone," she cried, "and I am here alone in this horrible place. He has taken away everything that I love, and you"—she pointed wildly at the monkey—"you are all he has left me!"

Parker, a straight, harsh, grey figure, came down hurriedly from the upper story.

"God help us!" she cried. "What's the matter? What has happened?"

Mrs. Pierce-Dawnay flung her arms round the faithful woman's neck, and burst into a passion of sobbing.

"Ah, my dear, my poor dear lady!" she murmured. "Are there none of them left but me to take care of you? Come away, ma'am, come away! You're worn to death with all this silly turmoil and worry. Come upstairs with me quietly to your room. There, just what I always say; you can't put dependence on any man! That feather-headed old sawney, Antonio, promised me he'd be sure to be here to meet you, and take down the boxes."

CHAPTER IV.

TELLING OF LEISURE, OF LOVE, AND OF A SUNDAY EVENING.

The afternoon sun was warm on the high red-brick wall; warm on the grey and rusty lichens that encrusted it, and on the hanging plants of toad-flax, with their rosy stems, round, shining leaves and delicate purple and white flowers, that had rooted themselves here and there among the joints of weather-worn masonry. It was warm, too, on the tall spikes of scarlet lobelia, white wind-flower, and summer chrysanthemum, in the broad border just below; warm on the southern front of the long, low house, with its rough, buff-coloured, stuccoed walls, half hidden under climbing roses, and its wide gables, with their carved clap-boards; warm on the upward stretch of ruddy tiled roof, and the two enormous twisted chimney-stacks above; warm, finally—pleasantly, soothingly, sleepily warm—on Philip Enderby, as he sat in a garden chair on the gravel walk, just in front of the flower-border, with his legs crossed, his hat tilted down over his eyes, and a half-consumed cigarette, the blue smoke-rings of which curled lazily out and up in the still air, between his fingers.

In front of him lay the level green expanse of a tennis-lawn, with bright flower-beds on either hand, ending in a gentle slope of grass, and a space of half-wild ground, such as our forefathers would have termed a pleasaunce,—planted with little thickets of hawthorn, yew, lilac, and laurel, and overtopped by several good oak trees, a couple of feathery larches, and a tall, dark cypress, a trifle lop-sided from the force of the westerly winds. On the left stood the house; and on the right, across a sunk fence, was a good-sized meadow. A couple of old stag-headed Spanish chestnuts, whose first withered leaves fluttered slowly to the ground, rose from low mounds above the levels of rich deep grass. The elms in the hedgerows, too, had been lightly touched by the golden fingers of autumn; a yellow bough, here and there, showing like a sudden leap of flame amid the otherwise dense and uniform foliage.

Away beyond the meadow, between the trunks of the further elm trees, were stretches of rolling pasture and gleaming corn-land, with here and there the blue shadow of a wood, or the red roof of a distant cottage or farmstead, breaking the long dark lines of the hedges. And over it all lingered the soft magical haze of the sunny September afternoon, changing the heavy midland landscape into a land of mystery and enchantment, gilding the wings of the gnats as they danced up and down, up and down—a foolish short-lived multitude—in the broad sun shafts, and painting the distance in pearly tones, as tender as the shades on a dove's breast.

Now and then, across the lawn there drifted one of those streeling milk-white gossamers; on which, like a cloud-enthroned angel in a holy picture, with a difference, clinging tightly, with all his many-jointed legs, sits a small spotted brown spider. Looking at him, you wonder how he first contrived to set his fairy boat afloat on this ocean of warm air; but you may just go on wondering, for no one can answer the question. Only, like some wise Epicurean, careless alike of past and future, calm, and satisfied with that only true possession—the immediate present—the little, brown spider drifts on over flowers, and turf, and fruitful hedgerows, in the pensive autumnal sunshine, he knows not whither.

A congregation of house-sparrows, with short stout legs and hopelessly vulgar figures, chased each other in and out of half a dozen deserted swallows' nests, under the house-eaves, amid much noise and pertinacious chatter. While above, on the coping of one of the twisted chimneys, a respectable cock starling, his beak full of the mutilated remains of a large beetle, stood swearing horribly, anxiously desiring to present this appetizing morsel to his nestfull of dirty children, who squealed to him from a cranny in the brickwork close by.

and yet fearing to reveal their already far too conspicuous dwelling-place to the Colonel, quietly smoking his cigarette in the garden.

The whole scene was a peaceful and pleasant one, and Philip was quite in the humour to relish it. He had an agreeable sense of physical and spiritual well-being. A long tramp over the stubble fields yesterday, at Bassett, after partridges, and the mildly soporific influences of a Sunday afternoon, following on a well-spent Sunday morning, produced in him a condition of amiable quiescence, which rendered sitting still there in the sunshine, and looking silently at the garden and the country, the quick glancing life of the birds, and measured movements of the cattle in the meadow, a peculiarly congenial occupation. He felt that the lines had fallen to him in pleasant places. He was content; and, good heavens! how very much that means. Life had given him all he had asked for in the last few months, and he was simply fearlessly thankful. Like the philosophic spider, he floated along in a serene untroubled spirit upon his thread of gossamer. The present was surely enough for him. The present just now, indeed, seemed exquisite.

For, to tell the truth, Colonel Enderby's outlook had altered radically since the dreary evening—less than a year ago—when he had waited fruitlessly for his dying father's summons, in the silent house at Bassett Darcy. He had eaten freely of the fruit of love since then; and the taste of it had awakened the hopes, and instincts, and dreams of his early manhood again. It is not for me to say whether this move on his part was a progressive or retrogressive one; I gladly leave the delivering of judgment to others, and stick to my plain business of reporter. Anyhow, it is certain that the Colonel had grown tired of his old occupations—tired of war, with all its undoubted horror, and somewhat questionable glory; tired of fighting and marching; of the boom of cannon and crackle of musketry: and, still more, tired of peace; of Aldershot and its wide encircling moors, dark with fir trees, and sere with heather; tired of barracks and gossipy garrison towns, of endless military shop and bottomless military grievances; tired, too, of tropic Indian suns and biting Canadian winters; tired, in short, of all the pomp and circumstance of our invincible British army. It would seem that when Colonel Enderby married his charming wife, he somehow divorced his sword. He developed an unconquerable longing to go back home again, to settle quietly down among wide Midlandshire pastures, and to spend his days according to the simple, easy, uneventful pattern common to so many of his forefathers.

A considerable outcry had been raised when Philip announced his intention of leaving the service. His friends declared it was a fatal mistake; that Enderby had still a career before him, if he would only take the trouble to exert himself. Even persons in high places condescended to remonstrate mildly with him. "Colonel Enderby was too good a man to lose; he was so extremely dependable and trustworthy." But Philip had taken the bit between his teeth. There was a vein of sentiment in him, such as makes even the most reasonable and modest of men at times curiously indifferent to public opinion. He went resolutely, some people said obstinately, his own way.

So the Colonel turned his face homewards. He took the Manor House at Broomsborough, two miles out of Tullingworth, and about eight, as the crow flies, from Bassett Darcy. He rented a small farmstead, and some hundred acres of land; bought a pair of carriage-horses for his wife; proposed to get a couple of hunters before the beginning of the season, if he could afford it; and turned his attention seriously to questions of Cotswold sheep, pig-styes, and fowl-houses.

His brother, Jack Enderby, behaved very nicely at this juncture.

"Farming's simply the most rotten business out, my dear fellow," he said. "Believe me, you might just as soon put your money down the nearest well, or invest it in Egyptians. But if you really mean to go in for that sort of thing, you know, I've got a couple of first-rate short-horns I could let you have. You'll want some good dairy cows—they pay, you know, if you've got your market handy. Pray don't say a word about it—pon' my word, I want to get rid of them—it's not the slightest favour, I assure you. And there's a pretty little Alderney heifer too; beautiful thing, with a head like a deer, and splendid quarters—you'd better just let me throw her into the lot; she'd please your wife. Ladies like fancy cows, you know; short-horns are a bit too solid for 'em."

Another day Mr. Jack Enderby made yet further efforts towards the supplying of stock.

"I've got some uncommonly good pigs," he said. "You must just have a look at them. Pure Berkshire; you know my father always would keep them. Long and low, no leg to speak of, and a back like a dinner-table—make prime bacon pigs. But there's a prejudice against them in this country. I can't get any sale for them now at Slowby; though in point of fact those ugly tortoiseshell brutes they breed round here can't hold a candle to them. I'll send you over two or three to try. No, my dear fellow, for goodness' sake don't thank me. You'll do me a real favour in taking 'em off my hands."

Thus did the Colonel, metaphorically speaking, beat his shield into a ploughshare, and his sword into a pruning-hook; and, as he sat idly watching the gnats dancing in the sunshine on that quiet Sunday afternoon, he was very far indeed from thinking that in so doing he had been guilty of a mistake.

Presently the cock starling—who, after much noisy debate, deciding in favour of a bold policy, had delivered over the remains of the beetle to his hungry nestlings—broke forth into such a torrent of scolding, that Philip, roused from his vaguely pleasant reverie, looked up to see what was the matter. Across the short turf of the tennis-lawn Jessie came towards him.

The young lady had changed but very slightly during the five months that had elapsed since her marriage. She had collected a number of new impressions, and passed through a number of new experiences; but they had failed to leave any very definite traces on the brilliant, highly-polished surface of her personality. She still possessed the same gay humour, the same inimitable freshness, the same captivating quality; and Philip Enderby was still wholly devoted to her. He had not got in the least accustomed to her, though he had exchanged the relation of lover for that of husband— an exchange, which, alas! too often takes off the keen edge of a man's interest in a woman. The girl was to him as bewitching as ever. She provoked him into quick attention twenty times a day. He watched her as one watches the flickering reflections of running water on some bank by a streamside, delighting one with their endless change and motion and joyous sparkle. It must not be supposed, however, that Philip was fatuous about his wife; or that he fell into the tasteless and tiresome habit of praising her in season and out of season; of singing an everlasting hymn in her honour, and calling upon his friends and relations to join in the chorus. He was both too reticent and too proud a man to do that; and his love for his wife was far too deep and reverent a sentiment to have any inclination for flaunting itself in the face of outsiders. The girl's every word and look had an intrinsic, almost sacred value for him; but there was a vein of jealousy in his tenderness.

Jessie came lightly over the grass. In one hand she held her hat, and in the other a long narrow strip of bright-coloured Indian embroidery, which trailed along the ground after her—the end of it hotly pursued by a small black kitten. If the kitten found satisfaction in this form of entertainment, so, clearly, did its mistress. She drew the long web slowly behind her till the little creature was close upon it, and then, with a sudden jerk, whisked it away out of reach, far above her head.

"Look, Philip, look," she cried, in her clear sweet tones; "how charmingly he jumps;"—while the kitten, in a state of the wildest excitement, all claws and tail, sprung high into the air after its vanishing plaything.

The Colonel got up when he saw her coming, threw away the end of his cigarette, and stood watching her. He thought he had seldom seen anything much prettier than this fair, graceful young woman, turning and twisting hither and thither, within the circles of the gold and crimson embroidered scarf, while the black roundabout kitten leapt and darted around her over the sunny grass.

The kitten gave out first. It retired behind one of the poles of the tennis-net, sat down, and began licking its sleek fur with a fine air of indifference, as though nothing so trivial and transitory as the pleasures of a game of play had ever entered its small sooty head. Jessie cast a glance at it.

"Silly little thing," she said, "so soon to be tired."

Then she came on, and stood balancing herself on the edge of the turf, where it bordered the gravel walk. There was a touch of something curiously light and puck-like in the girl's appearance at times. Her face was deliciously merry as she looked up at her husband.

"What shall we do next, Philip?" she said.

Colonel Enderby smiled back at her. She was very irresistible in her inconsequent gaiety and endless readiness for amusement.

"What do you want to do?" he replied. "I am quite ready to obey you."

Jessie put her head a little on one side, and balanced herself daintily on the edge of the grass, swaying slightly from side to side, like a bird before it takes flight.

"Ah! but that is not quite enough," she said. "It will not do to obey merely. You must invent, you must devise, you must imagine."

"My wits are slow," he answered, still smiling. "I am afraid I must leave the inventing and devising to you, Jessie. I have always been better at carrying out orders than at giving them."

"The English Sunday is rather a trying affair," said the girl. "It leaves so little that one can do with impunity—social impunity, I mean. Here, in the country, they seem very old-fashioned on some points; and of course one doesn't want to make one's self different to other people."

Philip laughed. He made a rapid mental survey of the excellent middle-aged wives of his highly conservative neighbours, contrasting them with the young lady before him. The survey proved amusing.

"I am afraid you are different to most people, all the same, my dear little wife, without any making."

Jessie turned away, and began folding together the long scarf that still trailed behind her.

"Bertie used to tell me," she said slowly, "that I was a perfect example of the pagan spirit—that I was a most remarkable survival. It sounds rather well to be a remarkable survival, doesn't it? Is it that which makes me different to most people, I wonder? They are only themselves, I suppose; and I am a sort of re-incarnation."

Colonel Enderby did not in the least relish this somewhat occult strain of meditation. Then, too, the mention of Mr. Ames' name invariably aroused in him antagonistic feelings.

"Come for a walk," he said. "We will go down over the fields to the brook, and take a look at the beasts in the lower meadow."

Jessie put on her hat, and arranged her curly hair under the brim of it.

"Still it would be interesting to know whether I am really a remarkable survival," she observed quietly.

Colonel Enderby came close to the girl.

"Don't call yourself queer names, Jessie," he said; "I don't quite like it. When I said something just now about your being different to most people, I wasn't thinking about pagans or survivals, or any rubbish of that kind——"

"I am not quite sure that it is rubbish, you know," she interrupted, glancing up at him quickly.

"Yes, it is," replied Philip, with a certain insistence. "You are a very beautiful woman, Jessie; and in that there is no denying that you are pretty different to most people. But let us take ourselves and life too, simply and straightforwardly, darling, without speculating about ourselves, and trying to find out what's hidden. It's a mistake to do that. It makes people get all sorts of nasty unwholesome fancies into their heads: and when those fancies once take hold of them—never mind how untrue they were at the start—they begin to make them true, in a sort of way at least, by thinking so much about them. They begin to grow into that which they have brooded over. Put all that sort of thing away from you, Jessie; it's dangerous."

The Colonel spoke almost in a tone of command. He was a good deal moved; he hardly knew why.

A trace of surprise gathered in Jessie's expression as she listened to him. He had rarely committed the indiscretion of becoming didactic. "Is that all?" she inquired, when he paused.

"Yes," he answered, suddenly growing ashamed of his own eloquence; "that is all. I beg your pardon for preaching you an extempore sermon in this way."

"It was interesting," Jessie said, thoughtfully. "It suits you to be a little excited, you know, Philip. It makes your eyes a splendid colour."

"Pshaw!" exclaimed the Colonel.

He turned away, half pleased, half embarrassed by his wife's remark. He had always believed that his personal appearance was by no means his strong point; and any comment on it made him feel self-conscious and awkward. In some ways Philip Enderby was almost absurdly simple-hearted still.

"Come for a stroll," he said, after a moment's silence, without looking directly at her. "Let us go down over the pasture to the osier-bed, and I'll get you some of those big reeds with grey tassels to them, you wanted the other day for your jars."

So the two wandered away together in the still warm evening, over the ridge and furrow of the sloping meadow-land, towards the little stream. Philip was very gentle with his wife, very desirous to please her. He got her an armful of boughs, and reeds, and flowers; and told her about the different birds, as they called back and forth to each other from the high branches of the elm trees, or skipped in and out of the shelter of the thick hawthorn hedges. All living creatures had a strange fascination for Jessie; they seemed very near to her; she was never tired of observing them. Philip found himself talking very readily; he had been more pleased, perhaps, than he quite liked to own to himself, by his wife's little compliment; and the sense of pleasure had unloosened his tongue—he was unusually entertaining.

Coming home again up the field path, Jessie walked in front, her soft pale draperies brushing gently as she moved against the longer grass on either side the way. Down in the west the ruddy orange glow of the sunset lay along the horizon, promising another still, hot day to-morrow. To the east, above the upward sweep of yellow corn-lands, crowned with a line of dark broken wood, the moon rose, large and red, through a broad belt of dun-coloured vapour.

At the top of one of the long swelling ridges the girl stopped and turned round. She had taken off her hat, and stood there with her arms full of bending reeds and flowers, the upper part of her supple figure outlined against the evening sky. The Colonel stood below in the grassy furrow, and looked up at her. She was very fair.

"Jessie," he said, moved by a sudden

impulse, "are you happy? Are you glad or sorry you married me, and came away here to England?"

The girl laughed softly.

"I am as happy as the day is long," she answered; "and the days are admirably long here in England. There is plenty to do and see; I like having things going on all the time —little things, unimportant things, nice, cheery, everyday sort of things, you know. Now, this week, for instance, think what a programme! To-morrow, I must go into Tullingworth early, for some odds and ends of shopping—a hat, Philip; but a hat!—a simply ravishing hat! Then, in the afternoon, you drive me over to Melvin's Keeping. It will be rather slow, that garden party; but there is always the hat, *quand même*. Tuesday, you shoot at Claybrooke, and I go to luncheon. Mrs. Mainwaring's manners are delicious; they smell of dried rose-leaves and lavender, like her dresses. Wednesday, Thursday, Friday, something; —every day something, though I forget just now exactly what."

She threw back her head and stretched

out her arms exultingly, letting the reeds and flowers fall to the ground at her feet.

"Oh, I love this dear world!" she cried; "I love to be alive and young. If only these beautiful days could go on for ever, and I could forget that it must all pass and change. And yet if it did not pass and change, I suppose I should grow terribly tired of it."

Jessie shrugged her shoulders, and turned out the palms of her hands with a cynical little gesture.

"Bertie was right," she went on. "We are bound to get beyond one thing after another. But yet, it is very sad; why can't what is pleasant stay pleasant? Why must it always go on and on and on, in this dreadful way? The winter is coming to eat up our lovely autumn days; most of the birds will be gone, and those that remain will have turned into poor shivering little beggars. And I shall grow older and older; I shall get not to care for the summer and the sunshine; I shall not be able to be amused; and then at last I shall have to die. It must come——"

In a strong movement of protective love and tenderness, Philip Enderby came up to the girl, put his arm round her, and gathered her close up against him.

"Don't, dearest," he said; "for God's sake, don't talk like that. You're not like yourself, Jessie."

"Oh!" she answered, "it is nothing, really. It will all blow over soon, and I shall forget all about it. I don't often think of what is terrible. Only sometimes it has come over me lately that everything is slipping away, and that every day is a day lost out of my life, and I feel as if I should go mad. I cannot die," she cried; "I will not die."

Philip tried to speak, but she silenced him.

"You are devout; and people who are devout never quite understand, however kind they may be. They tell one about heaven; and, after all, what do they know about it? they have never been there. I want life—this life, which I know. I would rather go on living as an animal, a tree, as that soft, stupid little white moth there, settling down on the grass, than go away somewhere else, I don't know—nobody really knows—where."

She broke away from Philip Enderby.

"Oh, it is dreadful, dreadful!" she cried.

"Yes, it is dreadful," said the Colonel, "to hear you speak in this wild way. My dear child, you must stop. I shall have you ill."

He was utterly amazed, almost alarmed for the girl's reason—alarmed, too, at what she said. Life and death, heaven and hell, were matters which he had always taken very simply and faithfully. He was practically acquainted with the two first, and had never seen any reason to question the existence of the two second. To rebel against the fundamental constitution of things seemed to him little short of impious. Then, this sudden outbreak of Jessie's was so entirely unprecedented, so wholly opposed to her generally gay, light-hearted ways, that it fairly confounded him.

"Come home, darling," he said; "come home and try to think about something else. You are very young, you know.

When you grow older you'll get to take things more for granted; everybody does."

Jessie looked up with a strange little smile.

"I suppose they do; and perhaps that's the worst of it."

She stooped down and gathered together the fallen reeds and flowers. "Poor dears! we won't let them die before their time, anyway," she observed parenthetically. Then she turned her face homewards.

Philip walked beside her in silence. This resumption of her ordinary manner was hardly less confusing to him than her violent and causeless emotion.

"I don't know what made me think of all this to-night," she said presently, in her usual clear sweet tones. "It was singular. I rarely think of anything disagreeable."

As Jessie spoke they reached the little gate leading from the meadow before the house into the garden. The Colonel was busy with his own thoughts; he did not find the latch at once.

"Oh, how long you are!" cried the girl, a trifle wearily.

Philip held back the gate for her to go through. As she passed him he looked at her searchingly in the soft half-light.

Jessie turned to him with a smile as bright as spring morning.

"Poor dear Philip," she said; "you take things too seriously. Now, I get over my troubles in no time. They are gone, vanished —never to return, probably. I mean to have another charming day to-morrow. Oh, don't look sceptical; it's all over! Let us come in at once. I am so hungry; I shall be so glad of my dinner."

This last announcement was sufficiently practical, mundane, and consequently reassuring; but, all the same, Philip did not quite regain his serenity of mind. The completeness of his content had been shaken. The milk-white gossamer no longer drifted free, in happy, aimless fashion, in the warm autumnal sunshine. It was caught by a straggling branch and held captive, while the poor brown spider, his aerial voyage cut short, found himself unexpectedly called upon to reckon with new and slightly incomprehensible facts.

—And yet, at the risk of seeming to deal in paradox, I am inclined to assert that Jessie Enderby had never come nearer escaping from the inherent egotism of her nature, and rising to a worthier and higher spiritual level, than in that inconsequent and, to her husband, profoundly disturbing outburst of emotion.

BOOK FIFTH.

IN SUSPENSE.

CHAPTER I.

JESSIE ANSWERS A QUESTION.

It is very far from the desire of the present writer to blow up a trumpet in the new moon, call a solemn assembly, and loudly proclaim the virtue and wisdom of his own generation. We are not better than our fathers; in some ways we are probably a good deal worse. But, life being the highly confusing business that it is, and we ourselves being so pre-eminently unsatisfactory, it is the more incumbent upon each one of us to gather up a few stray crumbs of comfort wherever we can find them. Even the most rooted pessimist admits degrees of density in the universal disorder; sees points of less darkness; perceives here and there a struggle—though that struggle is doomed to be lamentably partial and transitory—towards the evolution of light.

Our elders deplore the disillusioned, unenthusiastic attitude of our generation; its unpleasing clearness of head, hardness of heart, and unlovely ability to take good care of itself. They say romance is dead, the shrines are empty, the gods are broken. We have cast down the image of Serapis, which they set up with so much hope and fervour, and have pointed to the rats scampering out of the body of their fallen idol with profane and idle laughter.

All of which is true, no doubt, in a measure. Only one would like to ask, who, after all, is to blame? You of the last generation bade us be free, hate cant, cease to mistake clothes for the man who wore them, love beauty, cultivate a scientific habit of mind,—and we obeyed you. We ceased to bow blindly before authority; we put a broom through the elaborate cobwebs of many a school and sect; we tried to examine the grounds of our beliefs, and deal with facts and not with appearances. With acute and patient accuracy, we analyzed your position, and laid a finger upon its inconsistencies and errors. You impressed upon us the duty of tolerance, of being wide-minded; and we are wide-minded to the point of doubting the difference between right and wrong. You begged us to worship pure reason, and cultivate the intelligence; and we have cultivated it to the point of universal confusion—until, in fact, only authenticated idiots, of whom, mercifully, there are still a very large proportion left, have any wholesome compelling, natural instincts to guide them. Women were encouraged to be strong and fearless. They are both; and, heaven help us! what a graceful and engaging spectacle they are in a fair way soon to present! Men were to abjure their native brutality. In some ranks they have done so, and stand forth a mild molluscous race, but doubtfully capable of fulfilling the command delivered to our first parents, to "replenish the earth and subdue it."

We have obeyed orders; and, alas! to those who gave them the result seems far from a happy one. Yet even here the saddest pessimist, if clear-sighted, may still perceive points of light. The individual, as an individual, independent of his accessories, has become more respected. The distance has narrowed between class and class. Beauty and pleasure are recognized as the right of the many, instead of the exclusive heritage of the few. The so-called masses begin to be taken seriously, instead of being pandered to in public, and in private treated as a joke. More than this, we have got, surely, a greater love of hard, absolute fact. In our loss of respect for personages, for the pomp and show of privileged human beings, every human being has gained in value. We have, each of us, only a certain capacity of reverence and sympathy; and if the said reverence and sympathy are squandered on the pains and griefs—comfortable ones enough after all, in the greater number of cases—of illustrious princes and very obvious heroes, there can be none left over for the "dim common populations;" for the hero in the shooting-coat or white slop and corduroys; for all the Jacks and Toms and ordinary plain-headed folk, who suffer but never rise from the ranks, whose hearts break, who agonize, who die and go out into the great unknown darkness without any court mourning or black borders to the daily papers.

We have gained this, any way—a sad enough knowledge, after all—that Tragedy needs no velvets and sables, no fine speeches, unheard-of miseries, or broad dramatic effects; but that she comes and dwells in pleasant sunny places, sits down at comfortable well-ordered tables, avoids extremes, and manages, quietly yet indissolubly and intimately, to associate herself with the average lot of the average man and woman. It is not necessary to get excited about her, to be rampageous or hysterical, or to make an outcry.

The last generation hugged its sorrows, let them fume and strut, was wonderfully interested and self-conscious over them; fancied it perceived a divine intention, and was somewhat puffed up with pride at being selected as a worthy object for the chastisements of the heavenly rod. We have none of these subjective consolations, unfortunately. I do not think we are aware, either, of much surprise or spiritual exultation in the face of trouble. It has grown a little too common in these latter days, and we have grown too quick in detecting its habitual presence, to be disposed to make much fuss about it; though possibly our pain is none the less deep and penetrating, because we have at moments an almost humorous sense alike of its futility and its frequency. What is sauce for the goose is also sauce for the gander; and in learning the relative value of things, we have had undoubtedly to relinquish a good many active sources of private support and self-satisfaction.

But it is high time to go back and pick up the thread of Philip Enderby's history—a commonplace history enough, I own; yet not unrelieved by moments of pathos, of brilliant hope, and of gallant fighting in the cause of that which seemed to him noblest and best.

One evening, early in the ensuing winter, the fog had risen as usual from the chilly bosom of the clay-lands, clung close to the face of the fields, and wrapped itself drearily round the leafless spinneys. Every twig in the hedges was garnished at the end of it with a quivering drop of moisture, which gradually increased in size till it fell at last with a dull thud to the sodden earth below. The cattle huddled together in corners; and the thick fleeces of the broad-backed sheep looked dragged down with the weight of the wet that soaked them. There is a brooding sullen silence on such days as this which is almost alarming. Nature seems deadened, sluggish, indifferent. There is no wind, no change, no movement; only the gradual swallowing up of dull diffused light by slow oncoming darkness.

Down through the village of Broomsborough—over whose quaint black and white houses the little grey church, with its broad side-aisles, seemed to extend comfortable protecting wings, as of a well-regulated hen over her brood of chickens—two men were riding home after a day's hunting. One of them jogged along cheerily enough, bending forward in the saddle, and holding his elbows high and square, with a considerable assumption of what is commonly called side. The other man, it must be owned, carried the marks of recent disaster upon him, and looked in rather evil case.

"I don't understand even now how it happened," he said, turning his head stiffly. "The whole thing was over in a couple of minutes. I was underneath and the mare on the top of me before I knew anything about it. That young fellow Colvin rides in a careless, hot-headed sort of way. He was within an ace of being right on to us; and then I think, Drake, it's extremely probable you'd have ridden home alone."

"It was a nasty fall," replied Mr. Drake, nodding his head and screwing up his genial countenance with an air of strong disgust—"uncommon nasty. Good people are scarce, you know, Enderby, and, upon my word, I should go and see Symes or Lanning, or somebody, and get thoroughly overhauled. You must have got a most infernal shaking, if you got nothing worse; and, in my opinion, it's always best to look into that sort of thing at once. One may get all wrong inside, you know, and then there's no end of bother if it's not seen to in time."

Mr. Drake delivered himself of these vague and bewildering physiological opinions with much verve and earnestness.

Colonel Enderby met them lightly.

"Oh, I must be pretty tough by this time of day," he said. "A hot bath and a good sleep, and I shall be as right as a trivet to-morrow. If I see a doctor, he won't be able to tell me half as much as I could tell him, and it'll only frighten my wife."

"I'd rather frighten my wife twenty times over than get myself wrong inside and not know it till too late," responded Mr. Drake, in a tone calculated to carry conviction as to the entire truthfulness of the statement.

"Wait till you've got a wife, and then perhaps you'll change your mind," returned the Colonel.

The observation had a certain finality about it, and Mr. Drake relapsed into uneasy silence, till in the clinging fog and growing darkness the two men turned in at the gates of the carriage-drive leading up to the Manor House.

At the door Drake bundled down off his big hunter, chucked the reins to the waiting groom, and began feeling about the other horse's legs in a knowing and scientific manner.

"William, you'll have to look after the mare a bit to-night," said Colonel Enderby.

He thought it would be easier to give his orders at once before getting out of the saddle.

"She's been down and lamed herself rather badly. I fancy she has strained her off shoulder."

"Very well, sir," replied the groom, with an imperturbable manner and utterly vacant expression of face.

"If you think there's anything much the matter, you had better send over to Tullingworth and tell Oldacre to come out in the morning."

"Very well, sir," said William again.

Philip Enderby set his teeth hard as he got off his horse and on to his feet.

"Bless me, I am stiff," he said.

Indoors, Jessie was lolling rather disconsolately in an armchair in the low-ceiled drawing-room. The room was hot, for she had piled up the fire till it glowed with a great heart of living crimson between the bars of the old-fashioned grate. With that quick sense of taste—taste meaning, I suppose, an accurate reading of the true relation between means and ends—Jessie had put aside all Italian conceptions of decoration, and had filled her English home with full dark colours, had laid down thick noiseless carpets, and hung the windows with glowing, deep-toned stuffs. "It must all look warm and soft," she said; "what you call snug. A house never looks snug in Italy; but there it is different; it is in the grand style. There the idea is to live in a palace, and let in the air and the sunshine. Here it is to live in a burrow and keep out the draughts." Jessie had certainly contrived to give her own particular burrow a most conspicuous appearance of comfort.

The curtains were drawn, and the room lighted by a couple of red-shaded lamps; on the girl's lap, as she sat in front of the great fire, was her kitten, curled round, with his shiny black nose pillowed on one ebony paw, in an attitude of profound repose. A piece of work and some books lay on the floor by her side; but just now Jessie appeared to be doing nothing. In point of fact, she had been dozing peacefully, and only woke up—with a troubled little start—when Philip's footsteps came slowly through the anteroom, and he opened the drawing-room door.

"Are you all right, Jessie?" he said, waiting in the doorway, and not offering to come further into the room.

"I believe so," she answered sleepily, without moving, except to put up one hand languidly and stifle a little yawn.

Something in his wife's tone did not quite satisfy the Colonel. He came on across the room, and stood behind her chair, leaning his hands on the back of it.

"Nothing wrong, dear little woman?" he asked, looking kindly down at her half-averted face and charming figure.

Jessie shrugged her shoulders.

"What would you have, Philip? I have been alone all day. The weather has been unspeakable. No one has been near me but the maids and Berrington. One is not intimate with one's butler, you know, and English maids have no conversation. I have been bored—ah! but bored. I try to read—one book is sillier than another. I try to play; but there is nobody to listen. Finally, Mimi, here, went to sleep on my lap. Cats possess a mesmeric quality; I went to sleep too. It was a relief, but it was hardly amusing."

"Dear me, what a dismal little history!" said Philip, smiling. "However, you see, I'm home now, and Drake's come too, to dine and sleep; so you'll have somebody to talk to besides the maids and the kitten."

"Mr. Drake doesn't like me." The girl spoke quickly.

"Drake's a fool, then," returned her husband. "But what on earth put that idea into your pretty head? Drake thinks just what everybody else does about you."

He sighed slightly as he spoke. Sometimes the Colonel wondered whether certain people did not think about his wife just a little bit more than they ought.

"No, he has never liked me," she repeated. "It began long ago, before we were married. I dare say he could not tell why, but I am certainly antipathetic to him."

Philip slipped his hand down off the back of the chair, and laid it for a minute on the girl's shining hair.

"What a magnificent word," he said. "I doubt if poor dear old Drake could even spell it. Now I must go and get myself decent for dinner. Will you get up and give me a kiss, Jessie?"

Colonel Enderby made his request humbly. He still approached his wife more in the reverent spirit of the lover, than in the secure and somewhat over-possessive one common to the British husband.

"Ah, will not that little ceremony keep, Philip? It isn't time to go and dress yet. I am so comfortable like this, and I don't want to disturb the cat."

Philip had a momentary inclination to consign the cat—in words, at least—to very warm quarters. He raised himself up suddenly from his leaning posture on the back of the chair. In doing so he was aware of such a keenly distressing physical sensation, that he could not help crying out. Jessie jumped up hastily, pushing the black kitten down on the floor with most unceremonious haste. She faced round on her husband.

"What is the matter with you, Philip?" she cried. "Ah, go away—you look terrible!"

The Colonel's breath came short and painfully. He bent forward again, and leaned his hand heavily on the back of the chair.

"Poor dear child," he said, "I am awfully sorry to have frightened you. I'm all right —only a bit stiff and shaky. Everybody is, more or less, you know, after a long day."

"I do not like this hunting in the least," Jessie exclaimed. "You are out all day, and it is very dull. You come home late, and look extraordinary; also, you get remarkably dirty. It is a sport for savages, I think, not for gentlemen."

"Say all that to Drake, at dinner, and see how he answers you."

Philip spoke with a faint attempt at humour. He slowly straightened himself up again. His face was curiously pale, and had a drawn look upon it. Jessie did not come any nearer to him, nor offer to help him. She stood aside, and watched him with remarkable carefulness and attention. Her smooth white forehead contracted as she did so.

"You are not going to be ill, Philip?" she said in a low voice.

"No, no, of course not," the Colonel answered quickly and cheerily. "I'm all right; I'm as sound as a bell, really—just a bit tired and knocked about this evening, you know; but nothing to matter, nothing for you to worry yourself about."

He came over to the place where the girl was standing, took her hand, and looked at her for a moment with a strangely wistful expression.

"Do you care for me enough to mind very much whether I am ill or not, my beautiful young wife?" he said slowly.

Jessie looked back frankly, sweetly, as she spoke.

"I care for you very much, Philip; but I dislike illness. Mamma used to want me to go with her and visit poor sick people, when we were in Florence. At certain seasons mamma was beautifully charitable. She would put on atrocious old gowns, and give everything away, and come home crying. It was very charming of her, wasn't it?"

"And did you go with her?" inquired Colonel Enderby.

He felt a sudden anxiety as to the tenor of Jessie's answer.

"Oh no," she replied. "How could I? I never go near people who are ill and may die. It is so distressing. One should only see people when they are well, and agreeable, and at their best. It is too much to ask one to see them when they have become—well, distasteful—I think. For the doctors and nurses, of course, it is different. It is their profession. But I dislike any one to be ill; it is frightening."

Philip Enderby turned somewhat sick. He fixed his eyes on the floor, and fitted his foot uneasily into the pattern of the carpet. They were rather a singular couple, standing there, before the glowing fire, amid the dim rich comfort of the pretty room. The girl, with her fresh dainty dress, and radiant youthful beauty; and the serious-looking, middle-aged man, in his top-boots and muddy hunting-coat, holding her delicate hand.

"A lot of things happen that we don't very much like, my pretty one," he said gently and sadly at last. "We must make up our minds to that. Only be sure of this, Jessie—nothing you don't like shall ever come near you as long as I can prevent it."

He stooped towards her and kissed her lips.

"There, smoothe all those lines out of your forehead. It's not your business to look troubled yet awhile. Leave that to those who are older and duller than you."

Jessie raised herself to her full height, and gave her husband a quick little trembling kiss in return.

"Philip, you are delightful," she said. "I have the greatest confidence in you. Now I will go and dress. I have a new gown. It fits to perfection. Even Mr. Drake must admire me in it. Bertie Ames always contrived, even on the days of neuralgia, to develop a compliment in honour of my new gowns."

"Never mind about Mr. Bertie Ames. He's far enough off now, anyhow. Go and get ready for dinner."

Jessie moved away.

"Ah! Bertie had his good qualities, though," she said, looking back as she went out of the door. "At times he was extremely entertaining."

When Colonel Enderby was left alone, he stood still for some minutes longer.

"Upon my word, I think Drake was right, and that I'd better see Symes. It was an uncommonly awkward fall. I'm half afraid, after all, there's something wrong."

He pressed his lips firmly together, and pulled first at one side and then at the other of his thick moustache.

"I shouldn't care a rap," he added, "if it wasn't for her."

CHAPTER II.

THE SHADOW OF A GREAT FEAR.

Everybody, I imagine, has a shrinking from putting questions which may lead, in reply, to the communication of unpleasant truths. Colonel Enderby did not go next morning to consult Dr. Symes. The weather for some days was wet and winterly, so he stayed at home with his charming wife, and thought, or tried to think, himself better. The stiffness, indeed, wore off to a great extent; and the bruises came out, as honest wholesome bruises should do, in various and sundry colours; and there, the Colonel hoped, would be the end of the whole matter.

His mental horizon was very fairly unclouded again about a week after his accident, and he began to entertain a contempt for his own pusillanimity in having given way at first to serious alarm. The weather had mended somewhat, and Colonel Enderby spent the first fairly fine afternoon looking round the farm, and superintending, in company with Essex, his farm-bailiff—a short, square-made, moon-faced man, rather weak about the knees—the doctoring of a bullock, down at a hovel in one of the outlying pastures, whose condition seemed to demand a vast expenditure of that unsavoury fluid commonly known as oils.

"If them red iles don't pull 'im through, nothing will, sir:"—after which comforting assertion of the attainment of the possible extreme of all human endeavour, the bailiff, stick in hand, and bob-tailed sheep-dog behind him, set off at a shambling walk towards the little red farmhouse, two fields away to the left, standing surrounded by its pale thatched ricks and dark buildings.

The Colonel was rather chilled, with waiting in the wet and slush outside the cattle-shed. He wanted to warm himself, and to get home quickly; he had been out later than he intended. Jessie might be lonely without him. He started up the rising ground of the pasture at a good smart pace. Some rooks, disturbed in their search for worms in the spongy turf between the ridges, spread their broad black wings, and flapped up reluctantly in front of him, to settle again a few yards further away, with quaint solemn hoppings, and recommence their investigations. The barking of the sheep-dog, and bleating and scampering of the sheep, as he hustled them down into a corner to be counted, came over from the next meadow, through the thick misty air.

Half-way up the long grass slope, Philip slackened his pace, and gave himself two or three good hearty thumps on the left side of his chest with his fist. He had got a nasty heavy aching there, and an odd sensation of difficulty in breathing. It was certainly exceedingly disagreeable; and the thumping did not mend matters appreciably. By the time he reached the top of the hill, and came to the gate opening into the road, just opposite the Manor House entrance, Colonel Enderby was suffering so acutely that he had to wait for a minute or two before he could recover himself sufficiently to cross the road and go on up to the house.

Once indoors, he turned into the dining-room, and sat down on the nearest chair. Berrington, the Colonel's old soldier-servant, now promoted—rather against Jessie's wish, for she could not get over the fact that his face was somewhat scarred with the small-pox—to the post of butler, moved about the room, arranging the table. The Enderbys had a little dinner-party that night. Jessie's little dinners were admirable. The squire and Mrs. Adnitt, with their youngest girl, Lucy, were coming over from Lowcote; Jack Enderby and Augusta from Bassett Darcy—Augusta Enderby, by the way, was an Adnitt, the eldest of that numerous family; Mr. Drake would drive out from Tullingworth to dine and stay the night; and finally, Ashley Waterfield, Lord Sokeington's brother, and his wife were coming —he took a house at Bashford a year ago, when he left the Guards, and got the adjutancy of the South Midlandshire Volunteers, and married the American, Miss Mamie P. Wrench, whose gowns and good looks made her something of a reputation in London for a couple of seasons. This lady had struck up a species of friendship with Jessie, based on the prolific subject of clothes, concerning which she was apparently willing to talk for quite unlimited periods.

Colonel Enderby sat down on the nearest chair, and leant forward—the position seemed to give him a measure of relief—with his elbow on his knee, and his chin resting on his hand. He felt wretchedly ill, nervous, shaken, partly by the actual pain, partly by the fear of what the pain might imply. He told Berrington to get him some brandy-and-soda, rather to that silent and fierce-looking person's surprise; for the Colonel was not given to "drinks" at odd hours.

After a time the pain subsided. He managed to get through the evening very creditably; though it was something of an effort to listen with intelligent sympathy to good Mrs. Adnitt's parochial woes; or to Mrs. Waterfield's remarkably voluminous information regarding her own tastes, habits, mental and physical idiosyncrasies, and those of her friends and relations, delivered in a high staccato, with the habitual communicativeness of her nation.

When at last the other guests had departed, and he found himself alone with excellent little Mr. Drake, in his comfortable smoking-room, a long silence fell on Philip Enderby. He stood with his back to the fire, with anything but a happy expression on his face.

"It's a pity that Mrs. Waterfield's got such an appalling, screechy way of talking," observed Mr. Drake presently, throwing himself back in his chair, and extending his feet towards the blaze. "I like a woman who's something to say for herself, you know; but, upon my word, she keeps going at a rate that fairly does for me. Seems as if she was wound up somehow, and let off with a spring. Yah! it goes through one's head like a steam-whistle."

Philip pushed his hands into his pockets, put one foot upon the fender, and leant his shoulders back against the mantelpiece.

"Mrs. Waterfield—oh yes!" he said. "She's a good-looking woman, but there is altogether too much of her for my taste."

He paused, raised one hand, and rubbed it slowly through his hair.

"You're always so kind and affectionate, Drake, I don't mind telling you I am rather in trouble to-night. I dare say it's nothing of importance, but I'm afraid I haven't quite got over that fall. I had such a nasty turn when I was out this afternoon; I can't make out what it means."

Mr. Drake sat up, his genial florid countenance full of kindly sympathy.

"I believe I'd much better have taken your advice, and consulted somebody at once. I'll drive you in to-morrow morning, and go to Symes afterwards. He's the best man, I suppose?"

"Excellent man—first-rate man. Talks too much like a book, you know; but knows his business. Well, as I said from the first, you ought to be thoroughly overhauled, Enderby. I see a doctor myself once every three months or so, on principle. Get a clean bill of health, don't you know. It saves no end of bother and anxiety."

If the speaker's personal appearance might be taken in evidence just then, one would certainly have supposed that he had reduced his private share of bother and anxiety to a minimum.

After a few minutes Colonel Enderby spoke again, with perhaps a studious air of saying something quite by the way.

"You'll excuse my asking you not to mention anything of this before Mrs. Enderby. I dare say it's nothing of importance, and of course I don't want to alarm her."

"No, no; exactly. I understand; of course not," returned the other man, leaning over sideways, and flicking off the ash of his cigar into the grate. "You need never be afraid of my letting cats out of bags, you know, Enderby. I'm the safest man in the world. If there's one thing I flatter myself I can do, it is holding my tongue."

And in this case, notwithstanding his proclivities towards gossip, Edmund Drake was as good as his word.

The dog-cart was standing at the door next morning, and Drake, having made his adieux, was fussing prodigiously in the hall over his coats and other impedimenta, when Philip went back into the drawing-room, to take a parting look at Jessie.

The Colonel was still in that initial stage of married life in which a man does not care to go out, even for an hour, without wishing his wife good-bye first. The habit is a pretty and wholesome one. For my part, I should be glad to see it last always, from the golden Jemmy and Jessamy period, right on to the quiet gray days of Darby and Joan.

"It is rather a nuisance your having to take tiresome little Mr. Drake into Tullingworth this morning," Jessie said, in a slightly injured tone. "Augusta asked me to go over to Bassett last night. There's no fog to-day. I should so like to drive. Must you go?"

Jessie stood just in front of her husband. She began twisting about one of the buttons on his great coat with her right hand, putting her head on one side, and looking up in his face meanwhile with a fascinating air of entreaty.

"The horrible fog has kept me in for nearly a week," she said. "Think of that."

It is never very disagreeable to a man to be coaxed by a pretty woman after this fashion. In his present anxious state of mind, Colonel Enderby was peculiarly open to the charm of his wife's little caresses.

"I must go," he replied, "because I promised Drake to drive him in, you see. But I'll be back as soon as possible. Have luncheon at one sharp, and then there'll be plenty of time to get over to Bassett afterwards. I ordered the cob this morning on purpose that you might have the horses in the afternoon, if you wanted them."

Jessie moved a step back, and regarded her husband critically.

"That is rather a good coat, Philip. I like you. You look very attractive to-day, somehow."

Perhaps it was very foolish, perhaps it was slightly pathetic, but at that moderate commendation the serious middle-aged soldier—who, by the way, had quite a number of decorations laid away in a drawer upstairs, the witnesses of gallant deeds—flushed like a girl with pleasure.

It is not wise to love another frail, faulty human creature as completely as Philip loved his wife. Yet which of us in our secret soul has not a sneaking admiration for such love; an underlying belief that, though it be an exaggeration, and a very provable act of folly, it is also more truly divine than the cold calculations of scientific, well-trained intelligence can ever be? Love on, then, dear fools! and we wise critics, while we stand safe on shore, replete with the conviction of our own immense good sense, and watch you drifting towards inevitable shipwreck and destruction, may still —who knows?—sigh a little enviously in secret, when nobody is looking, remembering that you, at least, have really lived, even though you have suffered; while we, perhaps, have done no better than play at living, after all.

CHAPTER III.

COLONEL ENDERBY MAKES HIS CHOICE.

"Of the existence of organic disease," said Dr. Symes, with his generous fulness of utterance—"of the existence of organic disease, from a period considerably anterior to the unfortunate event of last week, we have, I think, conclusive proofs. The acutely painful sensations experienced by you yesterday, Colonel Enderby, are sufficiently accounted for by the pre-existence of that diseased condition of the heart, and by the very severe shock to the nervous system consequent on your accident. You apprehend some distinct injury sustained at the moment of your fall, and of your horse rolling on you. You tell me you seemed to feel 'something go here' "—laying his hand on his left breast—" On that point

I cannot speak positively at present. Only time and observation will enable me to satisfy myself fully whether or not there is further lesion. You may ask me why, if, as I assert, organic disease was already existent, you were not conscious of it sooner? I reply that an affection of certain vessels of the heart may be present for a lengthened period of time, without causing any serious inconvenience to the patient; and that, as in the present case, a train of entirely accidental circumstances may lead to discovery. In other cases, it may happen that this discovery is not made till—though valuable to the medical adviser from the point of view of evidence—it has entirely ceased to be of moment to the patient himself."

"You mean that it's serious, then?" said Colonel Enderby, briefly.

He sat resting his elbows on his knees, and looking fixedly into the crown of his hat, which he had picked up off the table, and held in his two hands.

"I cannot, I regret to say, deny that it is serious," replied the doctor.

There was a silence. Presently Philip spoke again, slowly—

"I should like to know two things. First, what the immediate consequences are likely to be; and next, what you advise me to do."

"The immediate consequences, my dear sir, are, in great measure, contingent on your following my advice."

Philip glanced up quickly at the speaker.

"You must forgive my putting it plainly, but I hold every man knows his own business best. You may give me advice I can't follow. I must be the judge of that."

"Ah! my dear sir," returned Dr. Symes, blandly, "do you know that you promise to be rather an impracticable patient? We medical men are autocrats; we are judge and jury in one. We do not recognize the right of private judgment for an instant. It would be fatally subversive of our authority."

After making which decent protest, Mortimer Symes leaned back in his chair, with a fine professional smile, threw one leg over the other, folded his arms, and cleared his throat. The excellent man did not want to hurry matters. He felt a good deal for his patient. He had been very much taken with Colonel Enderby when he had met him the year before at Bassett, at the time of old Matthew Enderby's death. Since then he knew that the Colonel had made a romantic marriage. These facts, taken in connection with the subject of the present interview, made him hesitate before speaking his whole mind. His imagination was quick. He shrank from inflicting mental pain, just as, in professional matters, he shrank, unless it was absolutely necessary, from resorting to the use of the lancet and the knife.

Philip became acutely sensible of his companion's hesitation. He looked up again with a brief smile.

"You needn't mince matters, you know," he observed quietly. "I don't think I'm what is called nervous."

The doctor waved his hand, as though dismissing all such derogatory suggestions to the ends of the earth.

"My dear Colonel Enderby," he said,

"believe me, I am always scrupulously truthful, when I can venture to be so with safety, to my patient. In your case, I perceive that I can venture to be entirely truthful. I should be making a very poor return for the confidence you have done me the honour to repose in me, I should indeed be treating you with very mistaken kindness if I attempted to speak lightly of your present regrettable condition."

Philip winced. He had that instinct of pride which gives many strong and healthy men a sharp sense of humiliation, almost of disgrace, in the face of physical infirmity. He kept his eyes fastened on the floor, and began slowly stroking and pulling his moustache with his left hand.

"It would be highly reprehensible in me not to put strongly before you the gravity of the position."

Dr. Symes paused a moment.

"You must be extremely careful for a time. To begin with, I am afraid you must deny your taste for sport, and give up hunting for the remainder of this season."

"Oh, that's easily done!" said Philip, with an air of relief.

"That, I fear, is only the first of my unpalatable suggestions," continued the doctor, with an attempt at lightness. "Nature, Colonel Enderby, Nature has a marvellous power of adjusting herself within certain limits—of squaring her accounts, so to speak, even with disease. But her dictates must be obeyed scrupulously. She must be given time; be given encouragement; be met half-way. Her suggestions must be treated with reverent attention. In the present case, making myself the mouthpiece of our universal mother—if the phrase may be permitted me—I say that Nature prescribes rest. Rest is absolutely necessary for the establishing of an accommodation throughout the organism to morbid alterations. Rest is equally essential to the nervous system, as the only adequate means of enabling it to recover from the serious shock lately sustained. What do I mean by rest? Briefly this: a careful abstinence from all physical exertion; an equally careful avoidance of anything calculated to produce mental excitement; a relinquishing of all active employment for a time; and submission to the conditions—trying ones, I admit—of an invalid life. In everyday parlance, my dear Colonel Enderby, I must entreat you to go home and go to bed; and, moreover, to remain there till I can sanction your getting up again."

Philip rose, walked across to the fireplace, and stood there, leaning his elbow on the mantelpiece, and shading his eyes with his hand. This movement, notwithstanding his very real sympathy with his patient, gave Mortimer Symes, it must be owned, a moment of lively anxiety. He was a *connoisseur* in eggshell china, and close to the Colonel's elbow were some of his most valuable, and, consequently, most brittle specimens. They were in imminent danger, for the latter was evidently not in a humour to consider very carefully whether his action might imperil the integrity of such mere frills and fringes on the skirts of æsthetic civilization.

A horrible dread, which he dared not put

into words, which mentally he pushed away from him with an agony of denial and repudiation gathered and deepened, and threatened to overwhelm Philip Enderby. His wife's face—with its strange intensity and concentration of purpose—as she had asked him, amid the grace and comfort of her pretty room, whether he was going to be ill, came before him with a weight of meaning, with a suggestion of sinister possibilities that almost unmanned him. What had she said ? That it was too much to ask one to like sick people; that they became distasteful, and should, in short, be put out of the way; their existence was a blot, an offence, an outrage upon the fair face of life. How, then, could he go back to her, within an hour, and say, not "The sun is shining; we will go out and amuse ourselves;" but, "My dear, I am ill; I am going to bed for an indefinite period, and you have got to nurse me"? It was impossible.—Philip had a sickening sense that the very foundations of his happiness were crumbling beneath him. He turned almost fiercely upon the doctor.

"I can't follow your advice," he said. "What's the alternative?"

"The alternative? Ah! there—one moment, excuse me," cried the other gentleman, advancing with remarkable alacrity, and extending a protecting hand towards his cherished eggshell. "A thousand pardons, but it was nearly falling; a unique specimen too, unreplaceable. The alternative, Colonel Enderby? I fear it is a sufficiently distressing one. In all probability a frequent recurrence of your sufferings of yesterday, increasing in intensity, and in gravity of import. I must remind you that acute pain—I know by experience that I am not guilty of exaggeration, and I trust I need not accuse myself of inordinate cowardice—is extremely difficult to bear with calmness and resignation. It is irritating; I had almost said demoralizing."

Dr. Symes paused. The momentary fierceness had faded completely out of Colonel Enderby's face. He looked full at his companion with a thoughtful, questioning simplicity, which left the latter a trifle uncertain as to whether he felt the more disposed to laugh or to weep, as Philip said—

"Yes, I understand. It's not pleasant; but I suppose I shall be able to put up with it."

"That is not all, though, my dear sir, I regret to say." Mortimer Symes spoke gravely and quietly. "Suffering arising from the causes I have described to you is of a peculiarly agonizing character, and, if you are determined to know the whole truth, it is almost certain to terminate fatally."

Philip Enderby stood looking down at the floor for a minute or two in deep thought. Then he threw back his head with a sharp, half-angry shake.

"I must take the risk," he said.

"Ah! pardon me," cried Dr. Symes, "but positively I must expostulate with you. This is simply suicidal, Colonel Enderby. Rest and care, for a time, may restore you to a very fair measure of health."

"On your own showing something's hopelessly wrong. I could never be the same man again. No, no; I'm afraid it won't do."

Dr. Symes was deeply interested. He ventured one step further.

"My dear sir," he said, "consider. What right have you to chance the throwing away of a valuable life with this reckless indifference?"

The Colonel bowed with a certain dignity.

"Pardon me," he replied, "I have reasons for my action which I am not in a position to explain."

Then he moved across to the table, and picked up his hat and gloves again.

"I am very much indebted to you for being so open with me," he went on civilly. "I must get you to patch me up as well as you can, Dr. Symes, since I don't see my way to lying by just at present. A man of my calling and habits has a foolish hankering not to give in and own himself beaten, you know—to die in harness, as the saying goes. I will beg you to do me one more kindness, by the way, namely, to regard this conversation as strictly confidential."

Some ten minutes later Philip Enderby found himself standing on the doorstep of

Dr. Symes' residence. He regarded the broad clean roadway before him, and the trees and bushes inside the iron railings, forming the centre of the square, with curiously awakened attention. He watched William turn the dog-cart at the further end of the square, and stop the handsome cob neatly and accurately against the curbstone at Dr. Symes' door, with the sense of a man over whom a great change has come, who sees familiar objects with new eyes, and, as it were, for the first time. Henceforth Philip believed that a strange and painful presence would rise with him every morning; stay by him all day long; sit beside him at every meal; lie down to rest with him at night. At moments he knew that he would be called upon to bend every energy to conceal this hateful presence from the eyes of others, specially from the eyes of his beautiful young wife. The Colonel did not attempt to juggle or deceive himself, to soften down the edges of cruel fact. He looked his new companion steadily in the face; he wished to get accustomed to this fresh element in his life as quickly as possible. He had made his choice freely and irrevocably as he leant on the chimneypiece in the doctor's consulting-room.

There was a fine expression in Philip's blue eyes just then. He looked like a man who has taken a great resolution, and who walks forward, calm, undismayed, almost exultant, to meet his fate. Such hours are very splendid. They are touched with a magnificent daring and exaltation. But, alas! the measure of a man's true worth is not to be found in the sudden conception of an heroic idea; but in the carrying out of that idea, consistently, faithfully, through slowly accumulating days and months, even, perchance, years, when the glory has faded from the undertaking, when the freshness and the bloom have departed, and when the quick inspiration of an illuminated moment has passed into the silent continuous habit of a life.

When the Colonel, on his return home, entered the panelled hall of the Manor House, Jessie, ready dressed for her drive, was coming downstairs. The thin, delicate sunshine of a winter's day filtered in through the large heavily mullioned window on the turn of the staircase; warmed the full deep brown of the polished oak steps and banisters; and lighted up the girl's graceful richly clothed figure—projecting her shadow down over the stairway and across the intervening space of floor almost to her husband's feet. He stood still, and watched her as she came down, buttoning her long gloves, and smiling in her wonderfully radiant way.

This was a day of acute mental experiences with our friend the Colonel; and at this moment the experience took the form of a vivid reminiscence. He remembered accurately his first vision of Jessie, on the terrace of the little Italian villa, her simple cotton gown dyed rosy red in the shade of her great umbrella, her eyes dancing with charming vivacity, and the ugly chattering monkey by her side. There was the same effect of innocence, of frankness, of entire composure about her then as now. It came over Philip, with the force of a sudden revelation, that Jessie had not altered in the smallest degree in the last nine months; whereas he——? Alas! there was a whole age of difference between the comfortable middle-aged bachelor, who, in admirable bodily health, freedom of mind, and serene immunity from all extremes of desire, had driven—so unwillingly—those few scorching miles out from Genoa; and the man, who, now, with his heart torn between a passion of love and a black nameless fear, stood watching the fair brilliant woman, coming downstairs towards him. Jessie appeared like some embodiment of the spirit of life at that moment, triumphant in the strength of her youth and beauty.

"The sunshine does me good," she cried, throwing up her head and laughing. "It is a poor, second-hand sort of sun you have here in England; still, even so, it is delightful, after that abominable fog and darkness. I mean to have a charming afternoon. It is excellent of you to be home so punctually, Philip."

Her tone changed suddenly.

"You look very serious," she added. "Is anything wrong?"

By sheer force of will the Colonel pulled himself together.

"You look very pretty, and there is nothing wrong."

Perhaps Jessie detected something strained in the lightness of the answer. She observed her husband attentively. Just then Berrington set open the dining-room door.

"Luncheon's ready, sir," he said, as he came forward to help his master off with his great coat.

The meal was rather a silent one; Philip had not much appetite. As soon as the man-servant went out of the room, he left his place, and, drawing a chair forward, sat down by his wife's side at the head of the table. She turned to him gaily.

"It is going to be a delicious afternoon. The carriage ought to be round almost directly."

Philip looked very earnestly at her. Her face was wonderfully pure and childlike under the sweeping lines of her somewhat fantastic hat.—The young lady, by the way, had a remarkable gift of effective and picturesque dressing.

"Look here, Jessie," he said, "you like presents, and I don't believe I've given you anything for ever so long. There, hold out your dear little hand. I brought you home a fairing from Tullingworth this morning. You must wear it always, and, whenever you look at it, let it speak to you of my love."

As he spoke, the Colonel slipped a thick pearl ring on the girl's outstretched finger.

Jessie first looked down at the ring, and then up at her husband.

"Ah, it is ravishing!" she cried, in accents of genuine pleasure. "'Always' is rather a tremendous word, though, Philip; it seems to mean so much."

Then she fell to admiring her ring again.

Colonel Enderby smiled sadly.

"Perhaps my love for you means a good deal too," he said. "Jessie, listen. Let this ring be what is called a token to you.—You know, we can't quite tell what may happen; we can't see on into the future. If ever things go a little wrong, if I seem dull and silent at times, and don't quite please you—this is to remind you that, whatever comes, my love for you is absolute, unwavering, the strongest, truest, deepest purpose of my life.—Jessie, darling, sweet wife, promise you will never doubt me."

He had spoken quietly enough at first; but with the last few words his voice trembled and broke. Jessie stared at him with a growing expression of alarm.

"Something is the matter, Philip," she cried, shrinking away from him—"something is the matter! Oh, don't let me be disappointed—don't let it all get sad. I can't bear what is sad."

Certainly, as Mrs. Pierce-Dawnay had felt, there was something strangely baffling and perplexing at moments about this glittering young creature—something almost inhuman in her wild dismay at the touch of the sterner aspects of existence.

She clasped her hands with a swift passion of entreaty.

"Oh! tell me there is nothing the matter, Philip," she pleaded. "It is so cruel to let me be frightened. I was so happy, and now it seems all spoilt."

Colonel Enderby was at his wits' end.

He was frightened too, in a way; but he took the girl's two hands in his, and soothed and petted her, saying something, anything, he did not care what, so long as he could banish that strange look of dread from her face, and ring of unreasoning terror from her utterance.

After all, the Colonel and his wife drove over to Bassett Darcy that afternoon. The sharp trot of the horses, the keen frosty air, the pale, winter sunshine, the rapturous but respectful greeting of Jack Enderby's squadron of cheerful children—who regarded their captivating young aunt much as a company of plain but liberal-minded sparrows might regard some gorgeous tropic bird suddenly alighting among them—did much to restore Jessie's ordinary gaiety.

At home, in the evening, after dinner, she sat down at the piano, and played softly, wandering from one plaintive melody and harmony to another, with a sort of regretful accent in the progression of sweet sounds. Philip was desperately tired. He lay down on the broad low sofa, at right angles to the fireplace, closed his eyes and listened.

Yet he had really got through the day better than he could have expected; he had had no serious return of pain. The horses had pulled coming home, at starting, and the exertion of holding them had made him feel queer for a little while; but, fortunately, they had quieted down again after passing Stony Cross and turning down that long, rough bit of road by Wood End, just before you reach Lowcote village. Jessie's playing, meanwhile, was very soothing. Philip made a return upon himself. He began to feel more hopeful; to wonder if his sense of the gravity of the situation had not been exaggerated. Doctors overstate danger so often; they take unnecessarily gloomy views. They are so constantly in the presence of disease and death, that their minds naturally overstep the exact limits of a case. They see more than is really there. No doubt Dr. Symes had done this.

Jessie rose at last from her station at the piano, and coming quietly across the room, sat down on the floor at her husband's side, and leaned her fair head back against the end of the sofa.

"Ah, that is nice!" she murmured gently.

To Philip his wife's simple exclamation gave a delicate sensation of security and repose. He reached out his hand, and placed it on the girl's two hands as they lay open on her lap. She acknowledged his silent caress, with a pressure of her cool round finger-tips.

Like all true lovers, the Colonel was given to look at his mistress's actions through a very strong magnifying-glass, and find in them all sorts of subtle and precious meanings, by no means perceptible to the casual observer. Jessie was almost always gracious and good-tempered, and what may be called superficially affectionate. She was perfectly ready to receive practical assurances of her husband's devotion, if they were offered with taste and discretion, and at a convenient season; but she rarely took the initiative. Perhaps a man with a wider experience of the capacities of the feminine nature might have complained a little, and accused her of having given, by her looks and bearing before her marriage, a promise of passionate feeling which she was somewhat slow to redeem. Philip's experience, however, was not extensive. He was contented to worship humbly at the shrine; to pay his vows devoutly, without any strong sense that benefits should be reciprocal. If the Madonna did wink her blue eyes and smile a benediction upon him as he knelt at her feet, he was filled with gratitude, and reckoned himself as the recipient of a royal bounty.

It followed, that when, of her own accord, his wife came and nestled down so near him, when she let his hand rest in hers, that Philip's heart grew light. With almost a movement of shame he recalled the ugly fears that had oppressed him earlier in the day. His doubt of his wife's generosity and tenderness seemed to him little short of a crime. He fancied that she had divined that he stood in need of comfort; and with womanly tact and modesty had taken this graceful way of offering him her sympathy. Colonel Enderby was tempted to throw himself unreservedly upon her mercy, to trust her utterly, and unburden himself of his haunting secret. The demand might awaken a deeper life in her; change her from an enchanting child to a noble woman.

At last, filled with a recognition of her sweetness, with a chivalrous desire to humble himself before her, and confess his momentary failure of faith, to tell her all his trouble, the Colonel raised himself on his elbow, and leaned over till he could see her face.

He drew back with a chill sense of disappointment. Jessie's eyes were closed, her breathing was soft and regular.—She was fast asleep.

CHAPTER IV.

DR. SYMES FINDS A CLUE.

It is hardly too much to say that his interview with Colonel Enderby supplied Dr. Symes with an additional interest in life. He was largely given to meditation, and his conversation with the Colonel proved a most fruitful subject of meditation. Dr. Symes was not one of those medical practitioners who, in their devotion to actual bone and muscle, lose sight of the rich social and domestic drama with which their professional duties so constantly bring them in contact. His science was touched with romance; the mental and moral aspects of the phenomena presented to him claimed nearly as much of his attention as the strictly physical ones. In short, he was very far from having reached that condition of high scientific abstraction in which the sensitive, striving, shrinking human being is merged in the mere case; and the delicate opportunity of psychological observation is disregarded in a calm and somewhat cold-blooded desire to add a fact or two more to the records of experimental physiology.

Perhaps the very wide difference between his own temperament and career and that of his new patient made the latter all the more interesting to Mortimer Symes. For the doctor, like so many men of an intricate and speculative habit of mind, was deeply attracted by simplicity and directness of character. To him it always appeared that there were an infinite number of excellent things to be said on both sides of every question; and therefore quick instinct and fearless decision in action impressed him.

His professional career, it is true, had been very successful; his private life, on the other hand, had not been conspicuously so, owing mainly to his inherent tendency to weigh, consider, speculate, concerning the situation, instead of taking his part strongly and promptly. Colonel Enderby's clearness of mental vision, and calm acquiescence in the consequences of his own action, seemed to Dr. Symes extremely admirable. He had protested as vigorously as he dared against the Colonel's decision; yet, from the artistic point of view, he derived real satisfaction from the spectacle of the other man's reckless defiance of pain and probable death. It must here be frankly admitted that Dr. Symes was reckoned somewhat unsound, unorthodox, and even dangerously eccentric, by the majority of his professional brethren. His respect for the free-will of the individual frequently struck them as a reprehensible error. Still, his practice grew and flourished in the town. And even the county—which is so conspicuously conservative in most matters, and cultivates a righteous horror of frivolous unstable little Tullingworth, regarding it as a Nazareth out of which no good thing is in the very least likely to come—even the county had, in the last few years, given very sensible proof of its faith in this able, if regrettably liberal-minded, medical man. It may be taken as an axiom in every calling, I imagine, that in proportion as you gain the confidence of the lay world, you are liable to lose that of the members of your own profession.

More than a week passed before Dr. Symes saw the Colonel again, and then their meeting was a purely accidental one.

Tullingworth is a clean, pleasant, little town. It is well-built, spacious, cheerful; and has an undeniable air of good society about it. Like various other watering-places that developed their local resources during the early part of the present century, Tullingworth owes much of its successful start in life to that very well-abused gentleman, the Prince Regent. And it has not been ungrateful, inasmuch as it has inscribed his name and the names of some of his well-known associates, on the corner-stones of its broad neat streets and squares of excellent houses. As the Emperor Julian in Paris, so the Prince Regent, here in Tullingworth, would seem to have left a measure of his spirit behind him. The place maintains a calm, well-dressed, and gentleman-like air. It is leisurely. It cannot dig; to beg it is ashamed—unless, at least, the begging can be done with discreet secrecy. It eschews all exertion, save of the lighter and purely voluntarily sort; it amuses itself with elaborate care and praiseworthy diligence. Finally, it might supply an emancipated intelligence with almost unlimited subjects for light comedy pieces.

Perhaps Dr. Symes was afflicted with an over-cavilling habit of mind; but Tullingworth frequently struck him as rather a narrow and inadequate resting-place for immortal souls, on their pilgrimage towards eternity. This thought was vividly present to him one day when he had been visiting a fair patient, who, in the midst of considerable ease and luxury, was a prey to all those miserable ailments that take their rise in chronic *ennui*. He had listened to the lady's recital of her woes with a flattering show of comprehension and sympathy; he had been diplomatic; he had acquitted himself in the delicate office of confessor with tact and success. To quarrel with the vague subjective distresses of dissatisfied womanhood would indeed be, for most popular doctors, to quarrel with their bread and butter! Mortimer Symes had no intention of committing so palpable an error; yet as he came out of the house, and looked up and down the vista of the broad white street, with its rows of highly respectable porticoed houses, for his carriage, he was conscious of a movement of contempt, both for the megrims of his patient and for his own time-serving in so humouring them. Just then he caught sight of the Enderbys' phaeton, standing on the other side of the way.

Philip himself was driving. The horses were fresh, and were disposed to give a good deal of trouble. Fretted by the frosty chill of the afternoon air, they fidgeted away from the side of the road; backed at impossible angles; and refused to stand for more than a few seconds together. A man is seldom seen to greater advantage, perhaps, than when he is successfully managing a pair of restive horses.

As Dr. Symes glanced at the Colonel he could not help nodding his head with a feeling of satisfaction.

"There, at all events," he said to himself,

"is a person who is not addicted to sentimental vapourings; who has a plentiful measure both of moral and physical courage."

Dr. Symes hesitated. He wished greatly to speak to Colonel Enderby, yet, under the circumstances, he was tenacious of seeming to put himself forward.

"I must just manage to have one look at him," he thought. "He is taking a great deal of exertion; I should like to see how he bears it. It is utterly suicidal—unless I made an absolutely inconceivable mistake."

So thinking, he crossed the street, with his short limping gait; and took up a position on the pavement close beside the phaeton.

"Good day, Dr. Symes," said the Colonel, briefly, looking down from his exalted height. "You must excuse my shaking hands with you, these horses are a bit troublesome. My wife's in there, calling on Mrs. Colvin, and she's been rather long over her visit."

Here one of the horses began to back and plunge with unpleasant violence.

"Sorry to leave you," he added, "but I must just let them have a turn, I see."

He gave the horses their heads; and they started off at a rattling rate up the smooth street.

Dr. Symes had made the best use of his time, and noted several little things. Philip Enderby had aged sensibly since he had seen him a week ago. His face was paler and sharper. A hardening of the lines of the mouth; a contraction of the eyebrows; and a rigidity in the set of the jaw were clearly discernible to the doctor's practised eye.

"He is suffering," he thought—"suffering considerably. His conduct is incomprehensible; it is absurd, unjustifiable. It ought to be put a stop to."

And yet how to put a stop to it Mortimer Symes did not see. Colonel Enderby, he perceived, was not an altogether easy person to deal with; his very singleness of motive made him unapproachable.

"It is intolerable that a man should sacrifice his life in this way," the doctor said to himself. He felt angry; still he was sensible of an undercurrent of admiration for this display of undauntable pluck. It possessed, in any case, the merit of originality.

"There must be something behind which I am ignorant of; some underlying and very potent cause, which I am not in a position to lay my finger on at present. Yes, it is decidedly interesting."

Just then the door of the house immediately behind him was flung open, and the peculiarly clear detached accents of a woman's voice attracted his attention. Mortimer Symes turned towards the speaker. He was sensible of receiving a very distinct impression. A slender, fashionably dressed young woman came with a light firm step out of the house and down the steps. Dr. Symes caught sight of a delicate profile, clustering, ruddy, gold hair, sparkling eyes, lips parted in a brilliant smile over white, even, little teeth;—in short, he beheld an unusually pretty person.

Jessie Enderby was looking back, and talking with considerable vivacity to the young man who came with her out of the house.

"*Et voilà tout!*—Ah, but where are my husband and the carriage?" she said, as she stepped down on to the pavement.

"If Colonel Enderby has got so tired of waiting that he's driven away for good, I shall not be very much inclined to quarrel with him," remarked the young man, half shyly, half audaciously.

His hands were clasped behind him, and he was bending towards his companion with an expression of the liveliest admiration in his pleasant, beardless young face.

"You do not know Colonel Enderby very well," responded Jessie. "His talents do not lie in the direction of desertion, I am happy to say."

The young man coloured. He was aware of having been betrayed into an indiscretion, and of meeting with an unexpected rebuke.

Dr. Symes, hat in hand, came forward, across the grey flags, with his most urbane and courtly manner.

"May I venture to recall myself to your remembrance, Mrs. Enderby?" he said. "I have just parted with your husband, he will return immediately. The horses had become rather unmanageable; I could not resist standing here and watching Colonel Enderby. His driving is masterly."

The doctor's long, queer, shaven countenance and grizzled imperial—above all, perhaps, his slight infirmity in walking—were not calculated to prejudice Jessie Enderby in his favour. Fortunately, however, the young lady was at that moment in an excellent humour, prepared to be serenely gracious to all comers—even if they limped.

"Ah, thank you," she said; and then added brightly, "I remember you very well. We met at an afternoon party of Mrs. Latimer's. You were not there, Mr. Colvin?"

As she spoke, Jessie glanced at the young man, who, having recovered from his temporary embarrassment, and nodded a greeting to Dr. Symes, had taken his stand with his back to the street, opposite to Mrs. Enderby, and where he could command a full view of her attractive person.

"No, I wasn't there," he assented.

"I do not pity you. It was, between ourselves, a tedious, a really desolating entertainment, was it not, Dr. Symes? Fifteen people were introduced to me. They all asked the same questions—quite a little catechism."

"This becomes extremely agitating," said Mortimer Symes, with unction. "I trust, Mrs. Enderby, I was not numbered among that reprehensible fifteen?"

"No, no, assuredly not. You were the sixteenth; you were the refreshing exception. That is partly why I remember you so well."

"I am greatly relieved," said the doctor.

"But look here, Mrs. Enderby, what were the questions?" asked the young man, keeping his eyes fixed on Jessie's face. It gave him great pleasure to watch her while she talked, somehow.

Jessie shrugged her shoulders the least bit in the world.

"Oh, they were simply *banal* those questions. They had not even the merit of being extraordinarily stupid. All my fifteen acquaintances said they believed we had lately settled at Broomsborough. I acquiesced. They hoped I liked it. I hastened to assure them I always liked everything when it was fresh. They suggested—some, that is to say, the more profound ones—that Midlandshire is an object for unwavering devotion; it is very valuable; freshness has nothing to do with it. I replied, I should be able to judge better of that later on. They asked me if I rode—alas! no. They observed that a move was 'an awful nuisance, don't you know?' Need I go on?" she added, glancing up at her companions. "The recital of these inanities does not strike me as very amusing, after all."

"The amusement lies not so much in the subject-matter as in the manner of its presentment," said Dr. Symes, blandly.

It must be owned the doctor dearly loved a phrase.

Jessie smiled, and, looking down, proceeded to arrange the bow of ribbon on her muff with one hand.

"When I came to the last of those people," she continued, "I am afraid I did not behave quite nicely. It was a stout old lady; her head was decorated with white lace and insects in metal; she was not very distinguished-looking; the sort of old lady, in fact, you feel does not much matter. I saw she was about to commence the catechism. I was a little impatient; I stopped her. 'Pray,' I said, 'do not give yourself the unnecessary trouble of asking. I know the questions by heart. I do not stand on ceremony. I will tell you everything.' I did tell her," continued the girl, with an air of childlike innocence. "I fancy she is still under the impression I am slightly insane. I heard her say something afterwards about the strange behaviour of half-foreigners.—Ah! there is the carriage, though, at last."

As she finished speaking, Colonel Enderby drew up by the curb-stone. There was a singular effect of abstraction in his bearing —of tension, as though he was consciously expending a good deal of energy, and as though his fortitude was heavily taxed. Yet his face brightened and softened as he looked at his wife.

"I am very sorry to have kept you waiting about here in the cold all this time," he said; "but the horses wouldn't stand."

"It was not of any consequence. These gentlemen have been kind; they have entertained me very pleasantly."

"Mrs. Enderby does herself an injustice," said the doctor. "She has supplied the entertainment; the kindness is exclusively on her side."

Young Mr. Colvin came a few steps forward, with his hands still behind him, and addressed the Colonel.

"I hope you're all right again. I did go out to inquire, you know; but your servant seemed to know nothing about it, and Mrs. Enderby was engaged. I've felt most horribly uncomfortable whenever I've thought of that fall of yours. It was the nearest thing in the world."

Dr. Symes did not wait to hear either the end of the young gentleman's speech or Philip's curt rejoinder. A kindly instinct made him turn to Jessie, with his most ornate manner.

"My dear Mrs. Enderby," he said, "will you allow me one of the privileges that belong to age, and permit me to ask you a favour? I have known the Manor House for years, and have always considered it as a rare little spot. I have regretted that its various owners failed to show an intimate appreciation of the æsthetic possibilities that it offers. I hear on all sides, if you will pardon my saying so, that you have exhibited the most admirable taste and skill in developing those possibilities; that you have grasped the artistic idea of the old house, so to speak, and given the *genius loci* its opportunity; that, in short, you have created a delightful interior."

The doctor bowed.

"Will you give me leave to come and call on you, my dear madam? Will you reintroduce me to the dear old Manor House, now that it has, at last, had the happiness to pass into the hands of a truly appreciative mistress?"

Dr. Symes had an agreeable conviction of having succeeded completely in occupying Jessie Enderby's attention. She smiled very graciously, as she answered—

"By all means come and see me. I am very ignorant; I only know what I like. My house is an attempt merely; but, such as it is, I shall be delighted to show it to you."

"Jessie," said the Colonel, throwing back the rug that covered the vacant seat beside him, "are you ready? The horses will get fidgety again if we keep them standing."

Colvin made a hasty movement, proffering assistance; but the young lady did not accept it. She stepped lightly into the carriage.

"I find I always help myself best," she said, with a little friendly bow, as she settled herself into her place; while her husband, holding the reins in one hand, leaned across and tucked the rug round her. The young man drew back, evidently a trifle disconcerted.

Colonel Enderby nodded to Dr. Symes, turned the phaeton round with a sweeping curve across the street, and then sent the horses on at a rattling pace again.

For a few seconds Mr. Colvin stood, with his hands in his pockets, staring ruefully after the departing carriage. He was a capital young fellow, the pride of his mother's heart—she was a Waterfield, a first cousin of the late Lord Sokeington—and an object of the warmest admiration to his two roundabout, good-tempered, lawn-tennis-playing sisters. He was blessed by nature with a very open and ingenuous countenance, liable to betray freely all emotions working within.

"Upon my word, Enderby's an uncommonly fortunate person!" he exclaimed, with an involuntary sigh.

Dr. Symes turned and looked at the speaker. He had just arrived at a conclusion; it was a highly disturbing one. He believed he had dug down and discovered the root from which the Colonel's eccentric action sprung. He fancied he had sighted the potent underlying cause.

"Our copy-books used to inform us—at least, in my youthful days they did so—among many other valuable and indisputable facts, Mr. Colvin, that 'appearances are deceitful,'" he remarked, with a dry smile.

Then he moved away in the direction of his brougham, waiting a few doors down the street.

"Drive to Mrs. Farrell's, in Grove Walk," he said to the coachman, as he got into it.

CHAPTER V.

ROMANCE AT A DISADVANTAGE.

Lamentation, mourning, and woe reigned in the house of Farrell. Master Johnnie, that precious and somewhat precocious hope of the establishment, was afflicted with a feverish cold. The poor child had really been seriously ill. Cecilia prayed, watched, agonized. Mrs. Murray did something more immediately practical: she packed up her boxes. The worthy old lady behaved on this occasion with her customary forethought and discrimination.

"In case of illness," she said, with a pocket-handkerchief crumpled in her hand, ready for action—"in case of illness, you know, Cecilia, I have always said the same thing. Let there be as few unnecessary people in the house as possible. They give trouble. It can't be avoided. They add to the servants' work; they increase the confusion. I needn't tell you, I hope, Cecilia"—here the pocket-handkerchief came into play—"how dreadfully painful it is to me to leave you and our darling little Johnnie at this moment. But I don't consider myself; I put my own feelings aside; I am ready to sacrifice myself to the comfort of your establishment. No, no, my love; don't dissuade me. I see the right course; let me follow it, let me follow it.—I have telegraphed to Emily to tell her to expect me to-morrow, for a week or fortnight. Poor dear girl! it's so long since I have seen her. Sometimes, Cecilia, I own I fear that, in my love for you, I am tempted to neglect my other children a little."

All this, no doubt, was, on the face of it, extremely becoming and considerate. Flourish, excellent old woman, like a green bay tree; your manners and customs are deeply instructive!

Emily Murray, it may be mentioned in passing, had married, some years previously, a young clergyman of unimpeachable morals, and strong evangelical proclivities. This good man did not, unfortunately, regard his wife's aged mother with any overflowing sense of veneration. He had even gone so far, on one occasion, as to remonstrate with her on what he was pleased to describe as " a sad want of the visible workings of grace in her heart; " and to remark, in the presence of his eldest girl—a surprisingly sharp child of about eight years old, who promptly reported the said remark to her loving granny—that Mrs. Murray's conversation savoured somewhat strongly of that wicked city, ancient Babylon, "which the Divine Mercy saw fit eventually," he added, " as we all know, to visit with great plagues and eternal reprobation—the just reward of its profane and worldly doings." This, not perhaps unnaturally, had caused a coolness between the mother and son-in-law. But Mrs. Murray was a person of experience. She knew that there is a time to pardon as well as a time to take offence. And it appeared to her that, if your appreciation of the things of this life is still pretty vigorous, the moment for forgiveness has certainly arrived, when the exercise of that beautiful virtue will enable you to escape decently from a house tainted with fever—which may, of course, be catching;—and remove yourself to a purer and more salubrious atmosphere. Mrs. Murray, therefore, proceeded to forgive her son-in-law. She buried the hatchet, and after, metaphorically speaking, packing her boxes with plentiful sprigs of peaceful olive, along with her best gowns, took her departure.

Dr. Symes was aware of her mother's absence from home when he so hastily made up his mind to call on Mrs. Farrell. For Cecilia the doctor had a great respect. He believed her to be an eminently unselfish, conscientious, and high-minded woman. Circumstances, he thought, had been woefully against her. Under happier conditions her nature might have blossomed with a refined and gentle sweetness. Even for Mrs. Murray he had a certain regard. Not that he was in the least inclined to include her in the same category as her daughter. It was the frank self-seeking, and plausible hypocrisy of the elder lady that made her interesting in his eyes. In every relation of life, Mrs. Murray appeared to him radically objectionable; but, from the scientific point of view, the doctor was conscious that he enjoyed her—she offered such a rich field for research and observation. At the same time, had she not been safely out of the way, adorning the respectable hearth of her evangelical son-in-law, Dr. Symes would have thought twice before going to the small house in Grove Walk on his present errand.

Cecilia Farrell, on her side, took a good deal of silent comfort in the friendship of her medical adviser. He had more than once been the means of saving her boy's life; and Cecilia's gratitude, though dumb, was very deep. Then, too, he treated her with constant kindliness and consideration; he understood a half-word—and that to a woman in a trying situation is often the very greatest of helps. On the day in question, when she came down into the little square sitting-room to receive her guest, Mrs. Farrell's careworn, anxious face assumed quite a cheerful expression, and her impassive voice took an unusual brightness of tone.

"It is so kind of you to come so soon again," she said, giving the doctor her thin hand, with its prominent knuckles and long fingers; "But it really wasn't necessary. Johnnie is really getting on now; and I ought not to take up too much of your time. I know what a number of other people want you. I'm afraid this room is very cold," she added, looking round in a helpless sort of way. "I have been upstairs with Johnnie, and they have let the fire down. Will you like to come up at once and see him? There is a good fire in the nursery."

Dr. Symes was very sensible of the chilliness of the room—a meagre unsuggestive apartment, with a bleak white-and-gold wall-paper, and cool, shiny chintz covers to the furniture; but he valiantly dominated his sense of impending discomfort.

"My dear madam," he replied, "at the risk of incurring your severe displeasure, I must admit that Master Johnnie's health was not my primary object in coming here to-day. I think we may dismiss any further anxiety from our minds on his account. Last time I saw him, I perceived that he was, thanks chiefly to your unremitting attention, in a very fair way to make a rapid convalescence. To-day my visit is exclusively to you, Mrs. Farrell. I wish to have a brief confidential conversation with you, if you will kindly spare me a few minutes."

The harassed expression came back into Cecilia's face again. Poor thing! she was always on the look-out for the cropping up of possible discomforts. She received her plentiful share of worries in the same patient and submissive spirit that the ordinary donkey receives its share of pokes and blows. The donkey does not rebel, it is true; but it develops a very excusable tendency to wince nervously whenever any person pauses near it with a stick in his hand. Cecilia had an instinctive perception that a stick, in this case, was handy somehow. She sat down with an air of resigned expectation.

Mortimer Symes selected the highest

chair he could discover, and established himself sideways on it, leaning one elbow on the back of it, and resting his other hand on the head of his walking-stick. The doctor's little arrangements frequently possessed a disturbing effect of preparation for very serious business. And indeed, notwithstanding the quickness of his sympathy and genuine kindness of his heart, there was a superficial foolishness about the man; an inherent affection for posing; for fine words and redundant phrases; a tendency to mount the high horse at times,—greatly to the disordering of his hearers' understanding,—and, giving rein to that somewhat annoying quadruped, permit it to career away with him over "antres vast and deserts idle" in the most surprising and Mazeppa-like fashion. He possessed two very different styles of address; which may be respectively described as a wholesale and retail manner. Just now, having been a good deal exercised by various little incidents during the course of the afternoon, the wholesale manner was in the ascendant. Flowers of rhetoric threatened to blossom with amazing luxuriance in the thin, colourless atmosphere of Cecilia's chintz-covered sitting-room.

"My dear Mrs. Farrell," he began, "I find myself between the horns of a dilemma —the exact nature of that dilemma I will presently unfold. My daily occupation, as you know, is to give advice to others; at the present moment I stand very positively in need of advice myself. In difficulty and doubt our sex instinctively seeks the sympathy of yours. You know the lines," added Dr. Symes, with a wave of his disengaged hand—

> "'Oh! woman, in our hours of ease,
> Uncertain, coy, and hard to please;
> When pain and anguish wring the brow,
> A ministering angel thou!'"

Mrs. Farrell felt bewildered. She liked Dr. Symes very much; she would have been sincerely glad to be of service to him: but she was not poetical. She found it impossible to view herself in the light of a ministering or any other kind of angel.

"I am very sorry," she said vaguely.

The doctor, however, was well astride of

his steed. He heeded not comments: he galloped forward.

"I may compare myself, Mrs. Farrell, to one standing on the bank of a swift and turgid river. In the water below me I see, so to speak, a daring swimmer, attempting to breast the current. I ask myself, Can he succeed? Knowledge, accurate knowledge, of the unfavourable conditions under which he has ventured on this hazardous undertaking, compels me to reply that he cannot succeed; that his strength will fail, and those ravening waters will infallibly engulf him. I am in a position to render him assistance; but that assistance is unhesitatingly rejected. I pause. I consider. I cannot save the man against his will; and yet, my dear Mrs. Farrell, my nature revolts against the cold-blooded inhumanity of leaving him to his fate. If circumstances render my offers of help unacceptable, I must search elsewhere for suitable aid. In this painful situation, a beam of light appears to shine upon the dark night of my difficulty; my thoughts turn instinctively towards you."

Cecilia's critical faculty was not highly developed. She was impressed by her guest's generous flow of metaphor. She was also alarmed as to what could possibly be about to follow on so considerable a preface. She murmured something civil in the way of recognition both of the gravity of the matter in hand and of the compliment to herself implied in the final clauses of the discourse.

Then, as frequently happened—a proceeding which his auditors invariably found vastly disconcerting—Dr. Symes suddenly dismounted, discarded the wholesale, and adopted the retail manner. Having, to put it vulgarly, blown off his conversational steam, he became a reasonable being again.

"I am about to commit an indiscretion, my dear lady," he said: "but, in this case, I believe the end may very well justify the means; then, too, I have the fullest confidence in your wisdom.—I believe Colonel Enderby's wife is a connection of yours?"

The colour leaped up into Cecilia's careworn face. The stick seemed likely to come down upon a remarkably tender spot.

She became painfully conscious both of looking and feeling very awkward. She was glad the light in the room happened to be dim and uncertain.

"No," she answered hesitatingly; "Mrs. Enderby is not a connection of mine exactly. Her step-mother's—Mrs. Pierce-Dawnay—second cousin, Bertie Ames, is a first cousin of mine; but——" Mrs. Farrell paused.

"Step-mother, first cousin, second cousin!" repeated Dr. Symes. "The relationship is a little intricate, a little difficult to grasp on the spot. Still," he continued, "in any case, you are very well acquainted with Mrs. Enderby; you knew her before her marriage?"

"Oh yes; I have known her ever since she was quite a little girl."

The doctor shifted his position, cleared his throat, and then spoke gravely.

"There is trouble before Mrs. Enderby—serious, very serious trouble, as matters now stand. But as yet the trouble is not irremediable, if she has a capacity for skilful action and sincere devotion."

The daylight was nearly gone. The gas-lamps in the street outside threw a pale, yellowish reflection of the two windows on to the opposite wall of the room, and revealed Mrs. Farrell's face and figure with distinctness. Dr. Symes looked at her attentively, hoping to gather some information from her expression. He felt curiously drawn towards Colonel Enderby; he would have been immensely relieved to hear that his brilliant young wife was devoted to him. But Cecilia's countenance told of little beyond deepening anxiety.

"What is it?" she asked hurriedly—"what is it?"

"It is this, Mrs. Farrell," the doctor answered. "Colonel Enderby is running great risk of killing himself—perhaps suddenly; perhaps slowly, painfully—by inches, as you may say—and I suspect he is doing it for his wife's sake."

Cecilia Farrell remained perfectly still for a minute or two.

Then she murmured, in a low, unsteady way, "How dreadful! But what do you mean? I don't understand it."

Mortimer Symes changed his position again; this time rather irritably.

"I confess I do not wholly understand it myself," he said. "The facts are simple enough. Painful sensations, consequent, he supposed, on a fall out hunting, induced him to consult me. On examination, I discovered the unmistakable indications of heart-disease. I told him that complete rest and careful watching for a time were indispensable. He swept my advice aside with a wave of the hand. He insists on entirely ignoring his physical condition. I saw him to-day driving a pair of spirited horses; he was looking ill, and it was evident to me that he was suffering."

Dr. Symes paused.

"Colonel Enderby inspires me with remarkable regard and respect. To return to our metaphor, Mrs. Farrell, I cannot stand by till the swimmer throws up his arms and sinks down for ever under the cold waters of death, without making one more effort to rescue him."

Cecilia's lips were very dry; she could barely articulate.

"Dreadful!" she said again, under her breath.

"I am bound by a promise not to mention this matter to Mrs. Enderby—nor, indeed, to any one else," he continued. "I have, in truth, compromised myself by relating the case to you. But my conscience exculpates me; I believe I am justified by the end in view. Mrs. Farrell, I think you are one of those women—Providence mercifully sends us a few in every generation—who are born to be their brothers' and sisters' keepers. Mrs. Enderby is very young; and most young persons are selfish. It is excusable, in my opinion. The vividness of their own sensations, their lively appreciation of the pleasures of this world, leaves but little space for careful thought of others. Their own cup is full; and one cannot, I think, ask them always to be peering into their neighbour's cup to see if by chance it is empty. Mrs. Enderby is very young, I say. She is alone here; away, as I understand, from all her relations—her natural counsellors, as we may call them. A few judicious words from an old friend like yourself might prove an inestimable blessing to her at this moment; might go far to arrest the uplifted sword of destiny."

The wholesale manner had come on again slightly.

"My dear lady, will you undertake this mission? Will you approach Mrs. Enderby? hint at the real state of affairs? make an appeal to her affection? open her eyes?—do what you can, in fact, to save Colonel Enderby's life?"

Mrs. Farrell rose and roamed about the room in a confused aimless sort of way. The doctor sat watching her closely. He believed in her; and it would, he felt, shake his faith fatally in the self-sacrificing instincts of womanhood if she failed him. He tried to strengthen his cause.

"I have thrown myself unreservedly upon your mercy," he said. "I am sure you will take my word for it that the situation is one of appalling gravity."

Presently Mrs. Farrell came back and sat down again. She had no ready powers of expression. Her sensitive soul was imprisoned in a torpid, unresponsive body.

Emotion with her took the form of a dull, numbing, yet penetrating ache, which could find no relief in appropriate action.

"I would gladly do anything, if I could," she said; "but I dare not—I dare not, Dr. Symes. I am quite the last person who can interfere."

"Ah! but," he answered quickly, "there comes a point when it is a duty to lay aside diffidence and superfluous modesty; when, in the name of our common humanity, it is a simple duty to interfere."

"It isn't that," said Cecilia. "I would do it willingly enough if it was anybody else; but I can't, Dr. Symes—for Colonel Enderby."

The doctor was both annoyed and puzzled. For a moment he lost his usual urbanity of demeanour, and spoke without exactly considering whether in his zeal for the Colonel he was not oblivious of what was due to his hostess.

"And why not for Colonel Enderby, my dear madam?" he demanded.

Cecilia Farrell had not been wrong in dreading the stick. It had descended in quite a series of sharp blows during the past quarter of an hour. Under this last and heaviest of them the poor thing absolutely staggered. She put her thin hands over her face, and doubled herself almost together. It must be owned that in this posture Cecilia's figure was not seen to advantage. She had a very long back; and a long back is a disastrous thing in a woman.

"We were lovers years ago," she said at last, very simply. "Men tell their wives about these things generally, you know, after they marry; and laugh over them. I have never laughed over it," she added presently, with a quaver in her voice: "and so I couldn't go and talk to Jessie Enderby. She might misunderstand my motives."

Dr. Symes was silent. Mrs. Farrell's confession seemed to him abundantly pathetic. He was shocked, too, to think what exquisite torture he must have been putting this unfortunate woman to, all unwittingly. He tried to arrange his ideas so as to frame an apology which should be at once soothing and respectful. But Cecilia spoke again before his preparations were completed.

"I hope you won't despise me, Dr. Symes," she said.

"Despise you? Good heavens! my dear madam," cried the doctor, heartily, "I honour, I reverence you. I cannot forgive myself for having caused you pain."

That evening, while Dr. Symes was sitting in his well-furnished library, trying to forget the disturbing incidents of the day in an interesting monograph by a distinguished French scientist, on "Some obscure functions of the Cerebro-spinal Nervous System," a note was brought to him, addressed in Cecilia Farrell's narrow pointed handwriting. This was the substance of it:—

"I have thought over what you told me this afternoon. I am afraid I acted hastily, and only considered myself. I am afraid I shall not be of much use, but I will do what I can."

Dr. Symes contemplated the note silently for a little space of time. Then folding it up, he threw it into a drawer of his writing-table.

"That is a really good woman," he said half aloud. Then he settled himself back comfortably to peruse the elucidation of the obscurities of the cerebro-spinal nervous system again.

CHAPTER VI.

"FOR AULD LANG SYNE."

It is rather dangerous to make a diffident, slow-natured person the present of a new idea. The idea, finding itself pretty well alone in the mind of such a person, begins to expand, to permeate, till at length it becomes almost unfortunately dominant.

Cecilia Farrell's existence was a cramped and monotonous one. The stock of ideas upon which she maintained it was very limited. It can be briefly inventoried in two words—Duty and Johnnie. To Cecilia's honour, be it repeated that Duty did hold the first place, and Johnnie came second. Dr. Symes had introduced a third idea into her mind; and, after a sharp struggle, she accepted it, because it appeared to her nearly allied to her primary idea of duty.

But once having accepted it, it began to assume many fresh and inspiring aspects; the process of expansion and permeation took place; briefly, the new idea possessed her.

After she had put her boy to bed that night, and despatched her recantation to the doctor, Mrs. Farrell found herself by no means inclined for sleep. She had got something to think about. She went upstairs and sat down by Johnnie's iron crib in her bedroom. The fire sent a broad glow upon the ceiling. The house was very still. There was a noise of bells in the air, ringing down at the parish church some half-mile away across the river. This was one of the practising nights of the Advent season; and the sound of the peal came fitfully on the wind, now loud, clear, hopeful, running joyously down the scale; then turning and ringing change upon change in an intricate pattern of sound; and then again dying away, becoming soft, uncertain, distant—sad, ghostly bells, ringing the dirge of days and dreams and aspirations long dead.

Cecilia laid her hand upon the counterpane of Johnnie's bed, and leant her head back against the wall behind her. The bells affected her strangely. They carried her back in thought to the picturesque old cathedral city where she had first met Philip Enderby; and all the unfinished romance of her girlhood unfolded itself before her. She passed again pleasant, sunny, summer afternoons on the broad river, that slips away seaward below the gardens and pretty dwelling-houses of the suburbs of the town; and, further inland, stretches in long, quiet, brimming reaches under the shadow of steep woods and between flat rich meadows, where the cattle feed or stand staring with stupid curiosity at the passing boats from among the flags and blue geraniums and willow-weed upon the low red banks. She paced again the quaint, winding, paved walks on the city walls, and felt once more that quickening of the pulse and happy rush of half-trouble, half-expectation, with which of old, at some turn of the narrow tortuous way, she had suddenly come face to face with her lover. She remembered every incident of the dance given by the officers of the garrison, as a parting token of gratitude to the rank and fashion of the town and neighbourhood, for the kindness shown them during their stay. She recalled, too, her interview with Philip Enderby two days later in the sitting-room of Mrs. Murray's house, with its tall windows looking over the city walls and the wide green circle of the racecourse below, to the sharp curve of the river, round a high wooded promontory, under the hard lines of the red-brick viaduct, and across miles of rolling country to the faint blue-grey ranges of the Welsh hills rising against the western sky. Cecilia remembered the little presents he had given her; and the long, somewhat untidy letters he had scribbled her during those two years of patient waiting;—remembered, too, how the arrival of one of these same untidy epistles spread a glory over all the following day.

But there, upon my word you and I have had nearly enough of this, sensible reader—haven't we? I own I feel like some ghoul or other unholy creature when I begin turning over a woman's little graveyard of love-memories in this way. They are such delicate, ephemeral, absurd little things, that one is afraid of touching them with clumsy, masculine fingers. They are dead and buried, I know, long since: and yet, as one reads their simple epitaphs, and perhaps inserts an inquiring, speculative finger under the crumbling boards of their coffin-lids, one has a sense that what lies within quivers and shrinks away in modest horror and anguish from the profanity of one's investigations. Let us leave them to rest in peace, then, and come back to the robust and burly present.

When Mrs. Farrell met Colonel Enderby again, there could be no doubt at all that he was very much occupied with another woman. The whole of the Terzia episode had been deeply humiliating and distressing to her; not that she bore the Colonel any grudge. Her own marriage, she held, had entirely cancelled any vow of allegiance he might formerly have made her; too, the idea of engaging in a competition with Jessie Pierce-Dawnay was manifestly ridiculous.—Cecilia admitted herself to be plain, middle-aged, uninteresting, with rather pathetic openness.

But now the scene had changed apparently. Sorrow, pain, possibly death, were ahead. She was not in the habit of looking on the bright side of things, and had accepted the darkest interpretation of Dr. Symes' statement. Her mind projected itself with intensity upon the situation, and she saw that, along with this gloomy prospect, came her own opportunity. She might now be of use; and to be of use —too often in a sadly blind and blundering manner—was the deepest necessity of Cecilia's nature. She sincerely believed she was responding to a call of duty. Alas! Cecilia, look a little further into the question. Those meetings and partings, those hand-pressings and kisses of long ago, take this affair somehow outside the strict limits of cold duty, I fancy.

But meanwhile the poor thing had a moment of strong exultation, as she sat stiffly on her hard chair by her boy's bedside. She would go and see Jessie; plead and reason with her; implore her to acknowledge the truth—painful as it was—and meet it bravely and lovingly. Never mind, if at first the young girl should be angry with her, and intimate in her neat, clear-cut, smiling way, that she, Mrs. Farrell, had been guilty of an impertinence. Just now Cecilia felt herself strong, daring, not to be baulked by anything. To set things right, and then to retire into silence and obscurity, seemed to her a rather splendid way of terminating her relation with her old lover.

The bells clashed together once or twice loud and clear. Then there was silence. Little Johnnie Farrell woke with a smothered cry, and sat up in his small white nightshirt, his face flushed with sleep and his eyes staring wide open.

"Mother, mother, are you there?" he called. "I've had a horrid dream."

Cecilia put her arms quickly round the little trembling figure.

"Yes, dearest, I am here," she answered.

Master Johnnie recovered himself with great promptitude.

"That's all right," he said. "I was most awfully frightened."

Cecilia laid her thin, worn cheek against the little lad's soft, round one, and pressed him nearer to her; but the child drew back his head.

"I say, mother, you're all wet and messy, you know," he remarked, with an air of considerable disgust. "I believe you've been crying."

She had not known it before; but now that Johnnie called her attention to the fact, Cecilia became aware that she had been crying a good deal.

"I say, mother, you must stop off that; I don't like it," continued the boy, in a tone of high authority.

Then, as his mother wiped her eyes furtively, he added, with the sublime egotism of childhood:—"And, too, there's nothing to cry for now that I'm getting better."

Cecilia's heart smote her.

"No, no, darling," she said; "there's nothing—nothing at all to cry for."

Master Johnnie, having exercised the hereditary right of the superior sex and admonished his womankind, curled himself comfortably down in bed again. His mother watched him for a time; and when at last the boy's quiet breathing announced that he had found his way back safely into the mysterious kingdom of dreams, she knelt down on the floor by the bedside and buried her face in her hands.

For Cecilia had begun to suspect herself, to question the purity of her motives. Her thoughts had been vain, self-indulgent, unbecoming; she had been proud, rebellious, self-seeking. In common with most genuinely humble-minded and devout persons, Mrs. Farrell's sense of sin was profound. Really, by the way, that same sense of sin is a very singular phenomenon; for in proportion as sin itself is absent, the sense of it seems to flourish in the human heart. Cecilia's life for years had been one long act of self-abnegation, and yet she felt herself to be very low down in the scale of Christian virtue; her faults seemed numberless and ever-recurring, her alienation from the Eternal Goodness overwhelmingly great. While Mrs. Murray, on the other hand, whose progress through this world had not, to put it mildly, been exactly that of a prominent and conspicuous saint, was by no means afflicted with any such consciousness of her own shortcomings; but trundled along towards eternity in a very fearless and light-hearted manner.

Mrs. Farrell remained a long while on her knees,—praying both for herself and for brilliant Jessie Enderby. She prayed for Philip too. It does not very much matter what she said. Mrs. Farrell was not a talented or eloquent person; and her prayers were probably confused and imperfect utterances, not in the least fitted either to adorn the pages of a religious biography or to be printed in some elegantly bound volume of private devotions. Still, such as they were, they brought her strength and consolation; and may, therefore, be reckoned as proving personally and subjectively fruitful, at all events.

Next day the idea was still dominant; but it had suffered a change. It had passed a night within the grim precincts of a puritan conscience; and issued forth in the morning no longer clothed in the delicate garments of romance and tender memory, but wearing the sober, ascetic habit of unadulterated duty. Cecilia had reduced herself to order; and prepared to go forth on her difficult mission to young Mrs. Enderby in the same sternly mortified spirit in which she bore the many and grievous burdens laid upon her by her affectionate mother, or administered nauseous medicine to the weeping and recalcitrant Johnnie.

She had decided to go over to the Manor House without delay. She therefore started the following day, directly after an early dinner, though the weather was bleak and misty, and the roads were greasy with mud.

Cecilia had an unlucky habit of perceiving things just too late. She was full of a solemn conviction and a strenuous purpose; and it quite failed to occur to her that an ill-shaped over-garment, boots unsightly with mud, and the general demoralization of the personal appearance consequent on a long wet walk, might injuriously affect her influence with Jessie Enderby. The children of light, with their pure, straightforward intentions, are very far, too often, from being wise in these trivial matters; and the nobility of their motives does not, unfortunately, prevent their finding themselves at a corresponding disadvantage.

Mrs. Farrell—a tall, hurrying form, clad in that most lamentable of all feminine garments, a round waterproof cloak—took her way by back streets to a quarter of Tullingworth that lies across the river, along the low ground, between the canal and a range of dreary brickfields. This region presents a marked contrast to the rest of the smart, pleasure-loving little town. It is a moral Alsatia, to which, by the law of social gravitation, all the human refuse of the place finds its melancholy way. Mean, one-storied houses open on to narrow, black wharfs and ugly cinder-paths, where bargemen and labourers loiter at dreary corners, and ragged shrill-voiced children angle for sluggish minnows in the slimy water, while the smoke and stench of the burning bricks fill the thick air. Dirty little shops maintain a feeble existence, with an attenuated show of attractions behind the panes of their dim windows. Only the public-house rises prosperous, cheerful, defiant above the dingy squalor of unpaved streets and lanes. Such places are altogether too common on the outskirts of even flourishing, well-to-do places like Tullingworth, for it to be incumbent on one to make much fuss over them: suffice it to say that they, perhaps, wear their most forlorn and forbidding aspect on a drizzling winter's afternoon.

It was characteristic of Cecilia that when asked to assist in parish work, she should accept the care of this uninviting district, which had proved altogether too hard a morsel for the other fair devotees of Tullingworth. Mrs. Murray had spoken her mind upon the question; and prophesied that Cecilia would get little besides fevers, fleas, and ingratitude as the reward of her labours. Of the latter she did, in point of fact, get a fair share. Her anxious looks, her cold, yet hesitating manner, were not calculated to render her popular. Only Dr. Symes, indeed, in his most florid of moments, could have hinted at her relation to anything in the ministering angel line. During Johnnie's illness Mrs. Farrell had, not without sharp twinges of conscience, somewhat neglected her unpromising district. This afternoon, which she had determined in any case to devote to the service of others, seemed a fitting opportunity for the paying of some visits already overdue.

Revolving in her mind how she should open her conversation with Jessie, Cecilia went hastily along one of the unsavoury lanes, without any careful picking of her way among the cabbage-stalks, rubbish, and grating cinders that composed the roadway; and stopped at the last house—a miserable red-brick structure, abutting on the unwholesome-looking, excoriated stretch of the brickfields. A slatternly woman stood in the doorway of the cottage, nursing a baby of some eight or ten months old; and two under-sized children, with thin pinched faces, played about on the damp mud floor just within.

"You've come down at last, then, Mrs. Farrell," said the woman. "I thought you'd got tired and forgotten about us, like the rest."

"My boy has been very ill," replied Cecilia, humbly. "I could not leave him."

"It's no use asking you to come inside," said the woman, pointing over her shoulder at the bare room behind her, while she slowly rocked the fretting baby in her arms. "The bit o' furniture went the day before yesterday."

"Went?" inquired Mrs. Farrell; "went where?"

"Went for rent. Nice place to pay rent for, too, isn't it? They left us a mattress in the back room, for me and the children to lay on o' nights, and that's all. They're pretty well pined, poor things, wi' the hunger and cold. The men took the blankets along wi' the rest, and there's nothing to cover 'em; so they might as well 'a had the mattress too, as far as I see."

Cecilia fumbled in her dress pocket for her purse.

"I am very sorry," she said.

"Oh, it ain't much use your being sorry," answered the other, shortly.

Then, suddenly, the poor creature sank

down on the worn grimy doorsill, and burst into tears.

"Before the Lord, I've done my best. But everything's been agin me, what wi' illness, and slack work, and one thing and another. I've come down, and down, and down. I said I wouldn't give in, and I ain't; but it's going a bit too far now. Sometimes I think the canal there 'ud be the best place for all of us. It's best to be dead—be dead, and out of it; there's no room for poor folks like us here in this world."

Cecilia Farrell was deeply pained and agitated; she tried to speak, but the woman interrupted her fiercely.

"Oh, I know what you're going to say. There's the Union. I know there's the Union, as well as you do. Haven't I fought up against it these months past; though I knew from the night my poor master was brought home stiff and dead, last January, it 'ud got to come to that at last? Don't you be afraid," she went on, looking up with a gleam of bitter humour, as the two children, frightened by her tears, pressed up

against her, crying, " Mammy, mammy : "—
" Don't you be afraid; I shan't do them
any harm. May be I love 'em just as well
as you do that boy of yours you couldn't
leave to come and help us a bit. They're
very patient, poor things, but they can't
hold on much longer. They'll begin to cry
for bread soon; and it'll go through me, and
I shall give in, and take 'em to the House."

Cecilia held out her hand; she had
emptied the contents of her purse into it.

" There, take it; it's all I have got with
me. Feed the children, in any case."

The woman snatched at the money,
looked at it, counted it, and then laughed.

" You're not one of the wise ones," she
said. " The wise ones give us precious
little but words we don't want. This 'll
keep us out a few days longer, and any one
can see the poor things here 'ud be a deal
better in the House. You ain't wise, but
I like you none the worse for that."

" Perhaps we can arrange something for
you," Mrs. Farrell said. " I'll do what I
can. I don't forget things. I'll come back
again to-morrow or next day."

"You're going now, then? Well, I don't wonder. It ain't very pleasant hereabouts. A lady like you soon has enough of it."

"I have to go to another house where there is trouble," said Mrs. Farrell, sadly, as she turned away.

"You needn't go further than next door for that, then," the woman called after her. "There's a sight of trouble both sides of this lane here, 'most all the year round."

Life seemed to Cecilia Farrell a terribly dark and mysterious business, and her own share in it sadly touched with incapacity and failure, as she walked through the dirty streets by the canal again, and, passing to the left behind the evil-smelling gas-works, turned into the broad well-kept high-road, with fields on either hand, and neatly clipped hawthorn hedges, that leads from the outskirts of Tullingworth to Broomsborough.—Alsatia has the decency not to obtrude itself upon the sight of comfortable, well-to-do humanity; it hides its ugly head in unfrequented corners. You need know nothing about it unless you want to, be it remembered.

The drizzling mist had deepened into unmistakable rain. Cecilia put up her umbrella, and bent forward as she walked along the road; while her cloak flew out in a great balloon behind, then, collapsing, it flapped in the rising wind, giving her long, lean figure the strangest and most ungraceful appearance.

END OF VOL. II.

PRINTED BY WILLIAM CLOWES AND SONS, LIMITED, LONDON AND BECCLES.

POPULAR NOVELS.

In one volume, crown 8vo, cloth.

GARMAN AND WORSE. A Norwegian Novel. By ALEXANDER L. KIELLAND. Translated by W. W. KETTLEWELL. 6s.

MY DUCATS AND MY DAUGHTER. By HAY HUNTER and WALTER WHYTE. 6s.

DONAL GRANT. By GEORGE MAC DONALD. 6s.

CASTLE WARLOCK. By GEORGE MAC DONALD. 6s.

MALCOLM. By GEORGE MAC DONALD. 6s.

MARQUIS OF LOSSIE. By GEORGE MAC DONALD. 6s.

ST. GEORGE AND ST. MICHAEL. By GEORGE MAC DONALD. 6s.

SEETA. By COLONEL MEADOWS TAYLOR. 6s.

A NOBLE QUEEN. By COL. MEADOWS TAYLOR. 6s.

TIPPOO SULTAUN. By COL. MEADOWS TAYLOR. 6s.

RALPH DARNELL. By COL. MEADOWS TAYLOR. 6s.

THE CONFESSIONS OF A THUG. By COLONEL MEADOWS TAYLOR. 6s.

TARA: A Mahratta Tale. By COLONEL MEADOWS TAYLOR. 6s.

THROUGH A NEEDLE'S EYE. By HESBA STRETTON. 6s.

WITHIN SOUND OF THE SEA. By the Author of "Vera," "Blue Roses," etc. 6s.

OFF THE SKELLIGS. By JEAN INGELOW. 6s.

HERMANN AGHA. By W. GIFFORD PALGRAVE. 6s.

DOING AND UNDOING. A Story. By MARY CHICHELE. 4s. 6d.

GOD'S PROVIDENCE HOUSE. By Mrs. G. L. BANKS. 3s. 6d.

CASTLE BLAIR: A Story of Youthful Days. By FLORA L. SHAW. 3s. 6d.

LONDON: KEGAN PAUL, TRENCH & CO.

www.ingramcontent.com/pod-product-compliance
Lightning Source LLC
Chambersburg PA
CBHW022051230426
43672CB00008B/1144